The Ring of Truth

Sacred Secrets of the Goddess

Almine

An Extraordinary Revelation of the Source of Power

Published by Spiritual Journeys LLC

First Edition May 1, 2007

Copyright 2006
MAB 998 Megatrust

By Almine
Spiritual Journeys LLC
P.O. Box 300
Newport, Oregon 97365
www.spiritualjourneys.com

Cover Illustration–Charles Frizzell

Text Design and Illustrations–Stacey Freibert

Manufactured in the United States of America

ISBN 1-934070-02-5

Table of Contents

SECTION 1—The Ring of Truth

SECTION 2—The Ring of Healing

SECTION 3—The Ring of White Magic and Power
(Also known as the Book of Creation)

SECTION 4—The Ring of Spiritual Warriorship

Closing

Acknowledgements

When I received the very disconcerting instruction that this book had to be in the hands of the printer by December 1, 2006, the previous book, *Secrets of the Hidden Realms*, had not yet been received from the printer. The news struck like a thunderbolt; it usually takes a year to finish a book.

But Hilda, Robin and Stacey rallied us all with their unwavering faith that it could be done. I am so grateful for the gift of their presence in my like. Thank you, dear ones.

Almine

Dedication

To the Mother, Goddess of all life,
the glory forever and ever.

Preface

As a Toltec Nagual, Almine is dedicated to a life of impeccability and the goal of setting others free from illusion. Whereas other wayshowers gather more and more students, she assists in creating more and more masters, freely sharing her vast knowledge. She has achieved the ultimate goal of the Nagual, namely, to conquer death.

The deep compassion this Immortal Master has for all life can be felt in her presence. Her writing and speaking come directly from Source, through complete silence of the mind. Because of this, she is a conduit for endless information, limited only by our willingness and ability to receive. y to receive.

Foreword

Belesh-vi trahur pelech varavi
Staubalechvi hures mananur
Kreshvi arunat spelavechvi staurut
Nun-hersh bastelelut treuch manuvach

Upon my instruction this book has been formed
The ring of truth must be felt in your hearts
I made all things new; innocence has been restored

Belevish parve uvatrefbi klaurach
Nun sterva strahur min hur sut eluback
Nishva perutvi, elu sklahva starut
Men hersh urva praunach berastut

May you know me as these words unfold
Feel my love for you and through the gifts that I give
For eons my face has been hidden from my children
But now it is the moment for all to see.

Yrech stranu uretvi elesh manurech…

Soon every eye shall see my glory…

Given by the Mother of Creation
28th October 2006

SECTION ONE

The Ring of Truth

I. The Changing Face of Compassion

In the previous cycle, compassion, or love (the desire to include) was the compelling attraction of lightworkers to those who represented illusion or undeveloped light. They wanted to help, to save, to ease the suffering where pain prodded others to change.

It was inconceivable to abandon those who were on the treadmill of illusion and its accompanying chaos and pain. It was a requirement that the more light we had, the more our responsibility to reach out, assist and include in our lives others who had lost their way.

Workers of dysfunctionality were equally compelled toward us. In fact, they came in droves until we were left wondering whether we had stumbled into a madhouse by mistake. We didn't have to look for them; they sought us out, compelled by an inner knowledge that we had something they wanted—something long forgotten. Was it integrity? Or peace of mind? Or the power that accompanies perception?

Whatever they found attractive in us changed when the previous cycle concluded. Because the old laws of attraction have

3

reversed. In the physical and with energy, opposites no longer attract; in fact they repel. If we therefore stubbornly cling to the desire to physically include light-retarders in our lives in order to help them, their hostility towards us will increase. They must reject us.

They are not abandoned, however. In fact, great assistance will flood their lives, as we now study ourselves in mirrors of sameness. This is how it works:

1. With matter (physical) and energy, opposites repel and like (sameness) attracts.

   1.1 In physicality, lightworkers now refuse to bring dys-functionality into their environments. As they embrace those of like mind, their mutual support increases their joy, peace, light and love.

   1.2 Light-retarders can no longer feed off lightworkers' energy and must grow on their own. They congregate with others who are just as dishonest, unscrupulous and vicious as they. This increases their discomfort as they have to face themselves in the mirrors of others having the same qualities.

2. With light and frequency (love), opposites attract and same-ness repels.

   2.1 This means that the more we increase our light and love by finding the joy of surrounding ourselves with a new light-family, the more light those who are in darkness receive.

   2.2 Lightworkers often used to speak of 'sending someone light', but if that someone dwelled in darkness, it didn't work. Now it will. And we don't have to 'send' anything; it is automatically transmitted. As we simply create a joyous life, the joy rushes to the place of least joy, to comfort the crying child or someone who has lost their way.

3. There is another form of energy called 'heart energy', which was activated by Mother in the new creation. Heart energy always exceeds a being's quotient of light and frequency by a small margin. She did this so its properties of like energies attracting and opposite energies repelling would be more dominant.

3.1 Our primary responsibility is now to make sure we live a path with heart; one that fulfills and uplifts us. In this way, we render the highest service to all life.

1.2 The Additional Three Directions

Although much has been written in both *A Life of Miracles* and *Journey to the Heart of God* about the four directions and the tools they bring to help us discern our reality, not much has been known about the remaining three: the directions of Below, Above and Within. This is because the creational codes for these three directions were lost at the very beginning of creation, at the forming of matter.

At that time, the Goddess of Creation planned to have an element of forgetfulness programmed into mankind, so they might explore the unknown through experience. However the Goddess of Form, who held the active codes, didn't understand this concept. Feeling that she couldn't participate in forming what she considered to be 'imperfection', she shattered the crystal containing the creational codes.

The only codes that were salvaged were the ones representing the four directions, which represent only the vertical aspect of the tree of life, the vertical depiction of life's blueprint. It is no wonder the mysteries and spiritual teachings on earth completely overlooked the fact that there is also a feminine, horizontal aspect.

While the Mother of Creation carries everything within her as potential, the codes for these three directions weren't expressing in Creation; the DNA codes within all creatures were incomplete. If one can understand and interpret only that which is within, how then could anyone fully express or utilize the gifts of these additional three directions?

The gifts they bear are the elements of light, love and original awareness. Without light's codes, the average person couldn't recognize the difference between a demon and a god. Without the codes of love, they couldn't feel the love the Mother of Creation has for her children; and thinking they had to fend for themselves, became self-serving. Without original awareness, humanity would follow any seeming authority or charismatic leader.

Now that the creational codes for these directions have been recovered, we can interpret and receive the potential which lies outside of anything ever experienced. The directions of Below, Above and Within work together in the following way:

Step 1. Information Comes Through the Direction of Within

Information received from that which is the unknowable cannot be cognitively understood or given. It concerns that which has never been experienced before. It therefore comes in impulses.

If the direction of Within is not properly lived, the impulses will be distorted. The direction of Within can be fully understood only when we have internalized the truth that our environment is but a reflection of that which is within us.

The mirror of our environment now reflects that which we express in ourselves. If we are workaholics, we attract other workaholics. If we lie to ourselves or to others, we attract liars. The things we find in the mirrors of our environment are what we are. In the same way, characteristics which do not appear in our mirrors are those which we are not expressing.

Someone who fully lives and understands this, changes his environment by changing himself. Only then is the direction of Within open enough to bring through clear impulses from the unknowable.

Step 2. The Direction of Below Expresses Instinct

The impulses prompt the instinctual nature to express. The feminine aspect of the Below expresses impulses much like an interpretive dancer; we just know it's the day for kicking off our shoes, kissing a friend on the cheek, wearing a red tie or no tie at all. The masculine aspect pushes the boundaries beyond where they've been pushed before; flying higher, staying up later, running further.

The impulses don't bother to analyze; they simply express without regard for boundaries. But as with all things, there needs to be balance. In this case, the balance is maintained by the higher mind, guiding from the direction of Above.

Step 3. The Nature of the Above Guides and Receives

The balancing factors have to come from the nature of the Above. The masculine aspect observes the meaning of the dance. Why do I feel like walking barefoot to work? Why am I refusing to do things in the old way?

The feminine aspect of the nature of Above holds the space of the dance within safe parameters. Yes, you could walk barefoot to work, but if you were to go into the board meeting like that, you would get fired. If you play your opera in the office, your heart will soar; but better to play it softly enough that it doesn't disturb co-workers.

Step 4. Passing Along Information

Impulses received from the Within (potential) are passed on to the warrior found in the North to evaluate whether they are appropriate to be expressed. The new information is now used to make life strategy decisions.

If the information needs to be acted upon, it will be given to the South (material life) to turn into experience; and potential becomes actuality.

In this new way, actions are based on trust. Everything in nature no longer fears that it might not survive. The reality behind that 'appearance' or 'form' was removed when, upon entry into the new creation, all beings as individuations were given immortality.

This means that as individuations, beings would no longer be absorbed back into the sea of consciousness between incarnations. The survival instinct, based on the fear of total loss of awareness and individuation, is now replaced with trust. Each being can stay individuated and grow with the cosmos, contributing in its own unique way.

1.3 The Reversal of the Directions

As we have seen, there is a very specific route that information takes in order to be acted upon in our lives. It if is potential yet to be explored, it comes through the directions of Within, Below and Above. If we encounter the unknown or the known in our environment, information also travels a very specific path.

It is helpful to know how it traveled during the preceding trillions of years of exploring illusion. It helps us understand better how different this new flow of information will be now that there is no more illusion.

Before, in the cycles that have closed, the unknown and unknowable were encountered without. Now they are encountered within. This applies in the instance of the cosmos as well as within each of us.

The Flow of Information in the Cosmos

The reversal of the flow of information within the cosmos is a natural result of the reversal of the directions themselves.

But what exactly differentiates the East from the West, for example? Each is a vast frequency band with its own specific frequency. The Toltec seers call them the great bands of compassion.

For the first time in two huge cycles of life, each of them trillions of years in length, we have ascended into a brand new creation in which the actual nature of the directions is transfigured. The very fabric of existence has therefore been irrevocably altered.

To signify this change in the way life will unfold, a great cosmic event took place on August 11, 2006. Gods for the seven directions were called from among the physical males who have gone into the God-Kingdom on earth. A primary god was called for each of the seven directions, e.g., the God of the West. Within each direction, two secondary gods were called, e.g., the God of the Direction of the West, and the God of the Energy of the West.

(See Fig. 1, Previous Flow of Information, Fig. 2 Present Flow of Information)

Previous Flow of Information
in Cycles that Have Completed

Previously the promptings of our hearts guided our destiny.

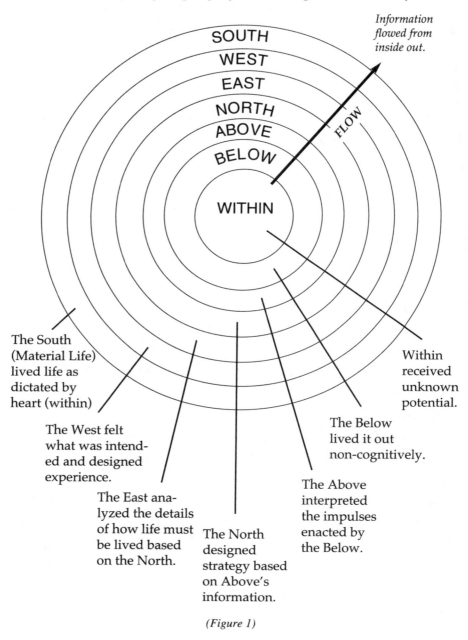

Information flowed from inside out.

SOUTH

WEST

EAST

NORTH

ABOVE

BELOW

WITHIN

FLOW

The South (Material Life) lived life as dictated by heart (within)

Within received unknown potential.

The West felt what was intended and designed experience.

The Below lived it out non-cognitively.

The East analyzed the details of how life must be lived based on the North.

The North designed strategy based on Above's information.

The Above interpreted the impulses enacted by the Below.

(Figure 1)

Present Flow of Information in Cycles that Have Completed

Presently we are creating how we want to live – there's no set destiny.

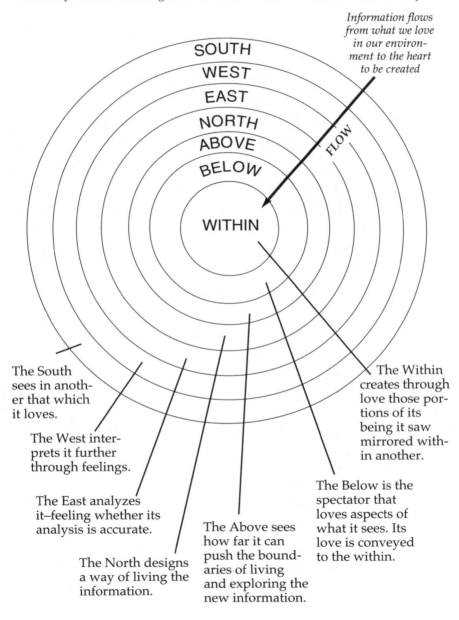

Information flows from what we love in our environment to the heart to be created

SOUTH
WEST
EAST
NORTH
ABOVE
BELOW

WITHIN

FLOW

The South sees in another that which it loves.

The West interprets it further through feelings.

The East analyzes it–feeling whether its analysis is accurate.

The North designs a way of living the information.

The Above sees how far it can push the boundaries of living and exploring the new information.

The Within creates through love those portions of its being it saw mirrored within another.

The Below is the spectator that loves aspects of what it sees. Its love is conveyed to the within.

(Figure 2)

How the Roles of the Four Directions Have Changed

1. The South – This is no longer the direction of the nurturer. The nature of the South is now masculine; and males will now be providing 'external nurturing', which is support. The South now studies the known by getting to know itself in mirrors of others who are of like mind and heart.

2. The West – No longer the place of deep feeling, the nature of the West is now masculine. It is the place of intuition, where mind in a state of expansion can study the unknown. The Ascended Masters now hold positions here.

3. The East – The angels, fairies, elves and others from the devic kingdoms have moved to the East in two groups. First the angels moved, then the lower kingdoms. The East is now the place of insight through analysis.

Because the devic kingdoms now have to play very important roles at a much higher frequency in the East, two new fairy queens have been created to govern the fairies in this very pivotal function.[1] They are:

Queen Varetabauravetmishbrisbami

Queen Pelechkravisbavi

The elf king, and his advisor who sits on his right hand, have also been replaced. Their replacements are:

King Kramavichpreshprekmava

Advisor Grabaluch-hespi

4. The North – The females of all races now represent the North. Here, external warriorship has given way to the inner warriorship that studies the known portions of existence and its applications. After all, there is nothing left to protect our boundaries against if we each live within our largest identity,

---

1. On Oct. 26, 2006, hundreds of thousands of elves and fairies came to earth from Lyra to serve in cosmic capacities.

as a being with a unique consciousness spanning all that is.

Whereas strategy and warriorship previously lived according to what was encountered without, the new way of warriorship is now designed based on what is found within.

I.4 The New Process of Discernment

The South: Identifying the Need for Discernment

The very first sign that something needs our attention or discernment, comes from the South as a physiological response. We feel it somewhere in our body as a tightness in our stomach, nausea or a tightness in our throat. It is a good idea to scan our day or interaction with others every few hours (or at least once a day) to find where we feel a constriction. It is a bit like combing our hair to find where the knots are.

The West: Accessing Information

Once something or someone is identified as needing our discernment, we empty our minds and ask a question. We then wait for a symbol to appear to provide us with a clue.[2] Before we begin, it is helpful to first establish what symbol indicates a yes and what symbol is the one for no. A fish (meaning 'things are not as they seem') is my 'No' symbol, for instance, but you will identify your own. When a symbol repeats, it is a confirmation, just like a 'yes'.

We then proceed with a line of questions and symbols as in the following example:

"Why do I feel tightness in my stomach when I am in my work-place?"

2. See Symbols vs. Sigils, 2.4

Symbol: A blue handbag. (You know Susan owns a blue hand-bag.)

"Is it Susan?"

Symbol: A blue handbag. (A repeated symbol confirms the answer)

"What is the problem with Susan?"

Symbol: A hornet. (Which is Anger.)

"Why is she angry?"

Symbol: Purple Teddy Bear (The symbol that represents you)

"Why is she angry with me?"

Symbol: Calendar and a present.

"Is she angry because I forgot her birthday?"

Symbol: Calendar and a present. (Confirms the answer.)

The East: Analysis

The information then has to be passed through the analysis process. Remembering when Susan became hostile, you can deduce that her birthday was about three days ago. But she has never given you anything other than a verbal "Happy Birthday!" Why should she then expect a present? All these facts are next passed to the Inner Warrior in the North for a strategy.

The North: Strategy

The Inner Warrior determines that a kind and gentle learning opportunity for Susan may be at hand, and that you are privileged to provide it. The strategy is that you go the extra mile, produce not only a beautifully wrapped present, but flowers, too. On the card you write: "I know it's not really your policy to give birthday presents, (this brings the situation to light) but I just had to let you know how much you are valued as a friend and colleague, and knowing your birthday is somewhere around this time, I wanted to give you my very best wishes."

Through this method of discernment, the potentially hostile situation at work is circumvented. Feelings of well-being are created instead.

1.5 A GLIMPSE INTO THE WORLD OF TOLTEC NAGUALS

The ancient Toltec traditions speak of the Toltec way as having come from the Mother of Creation herself. Mother saw that corruption of the masculine grids would occur, which would in turn corrupt the feminine grids.[3] She created the Toltec way to rectify the grids, the pathways along which information flows, to form the ideal template of spiritual warriorship.

The spiritual warrior always knew that the battle was one to dispel illusion and gain perception. Wielding his or her shield of impeccability, the warrior traversed a path that embraced challenge as a source of power and perception. But at the end of July 2006, the cosmic cycle of exploring the unknown changed to that of exploring the known. This changed the very fabric of the Toltec's existence and put to the test the essence of spiritual warriorship: fluidity, the ability to spin on a dime at a moment's notice and change direction if that is required.

What is a Nagual

Man is unique within the cosmos in mirroring the macrocosm, giving him extraordinary potential for power and growth. But within humanity there is a being with a rare and particular

---

3. Each species has a grid that carries instructions on how to act. These grids are arrays of lines along which light in the form of information flows. When these, as well as the ley lines, are disrupted, it affects trillions and trillions of beings.

The Seven Bodies of Man

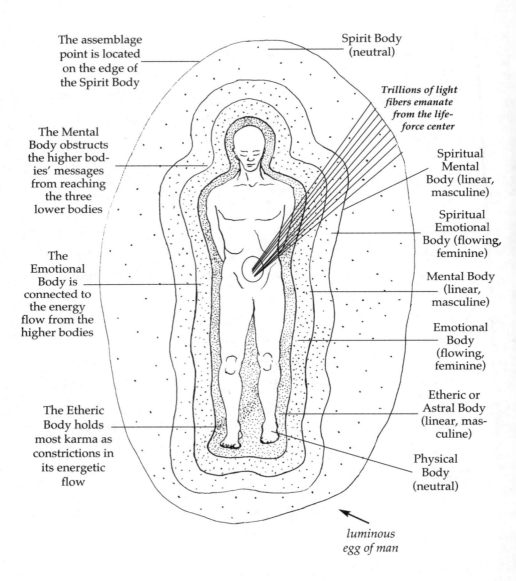

The assemblage point is located on the edge of the Spirit Body

Spirit Body (neutral)

Trillions of light fibers emanate from the life-force center

The Mental Body obstructs the higher bodies' messages from reaching the three lower bodies

Spiritual Mental Body (linear, masculine)

Spiritual Emotional Body (flowing, feminine)

The Emotional Body is connected to the energy flow from the higher bodies

Mental Body (linear, masculine)

Emotional Body (flowing, feminine)

Etheric or Astral Body (linear, masculine)

The Etheric Body holds most karma as constrictions in its energetic flow

Physical Body (neutral)

luminous egg of man

The bodies are superimposed over each other and form the luminous cocoon of man. The trillions of light fibers from the lifeforce center penetrate all other bodies forming the spirit body.

(Figure 3)

16

configuration of fields around his or her body that mirrors the macrocosm even more closely: the Nagual.

The seven bodies of man (etheric, emotional, mental, etc.) *(Fig. 3, The Seven Bodies of Man)* are stacked inside one another, forming a luminous cocoon which represents the cosmos. The Nagual, on the other hand, has a double luminous cocoon that represents not only the cosmos, but also the Infinite that created it. This enables him or her to hold a lot more energy, and with more energy comes more consciousness.

The Nagual has been dedicated to leading others to freedom from illusion—an ancient and noble dedication kept alive throughout more than a million years of spiritual history. But in one fell swoop during the last week of July 2006, the Nagual's purpose for existence was re-written. As the exploration of illusion or the unknown gave way to the study of the known, the Nagual's life became dedicated to embodying and mirroring that which most closely resembles the divine, that which is and which reflects the Infinite's being.

Three-pronged and Four-pronged Naguals

Unlike other light promoters, the Nagual undergoes specific mental and emotional testings that will crack the luminous cocoon, enabling more energy to be accessed and creating protrusions, or prongs, around the edge of the cocoon. Where three cracks branch out from one another, three prongs appear. Where two cracks form and criss-cross each other, four prongs appear. This creates what is called three- and four-pronged Naguals.

Three-pronged Naguals function much the same way within the cosmos as a fully activated pineal gland does within man, accessing the unknowable through insight. They don't always know where the information comes from, only that it's there and flows where intent directs.

The three-pronged Nagual can be of either sex, but is very much hermaphroditic in that the male and female components within are very evenly balanced. The focus or strong suit of this type of Nagual is the raising of the kundalini by the passionate inner love affair between the masculine and feminine pieces. In other words, the love affair is within.

Four-pronged Naguals, regardless of their gender, work in pairs. Each expresses a masculine or feminine aspect, functioning together much the same as a left and right brain.

The four-pronged Nagual who expresses the feminine gets symbols and feelings as non-cognitive information. Her partner interprets them cognitively, assessing where the gaps in the information are, and then re-directing questions back to her so she may gather the missing non-cognitive information.

These two (four-pronged) Naguals crack their luminous cocoons in different ways.

The Nagual expressing the masculine cracks his (or her) luminous cocoon by experiencing emotional turmoil so intense that it creates cracks in his fields (the fields do not crack all the way through, as this would cause death). The anguish he feels causes the fields around the body to spin differently and the cocoon cracks.

The Nagual expressing the feminine suddenly finds herself (or himself) in mental torture unlike anything previously experienced. Having silenced her mind completely at this point, she now finds she has a mental obsession. In the grip of what she knows to be a form of complete insanity, she nevertheless cannot escape the obsessive and increasing thoughts until, finally, her fields start to spin in an opposite direction and her cocoon splits.

The three-pronged Nagual, who expresses both masculine and feminine aspects, experiences both. After years of training that silenced all internal dialog and established emotional sovereignty, the Nagual now becomes obsessively needy. This causes increasing emotional and mental anguish and the cocoon cracks. This event is clearly recognized by Naguals to be what Christ experienced in the Garden of Gethsemane.

How the Cracks Occur

Around the human body there are sets of fields nesting inside one another (not to be confused with the various bodies of man). There are three star tetrahedrons (three-dimensional Stars of David), physical, emotional and mental—all occupying the same space. The physical one is stationary and the other two spin in opposite directions. The emotional one spins clockwise 21 times for every 34 times the mental one spins counter-clockwise.

Around these there are three octahedrons (four-sided pyramids set base to base). Again, one (physical) is stationary, and the other two (mental and emotional) spin in opposite directions—all occupying the same space.

When Naguals crack their cocoons during the human experience, it happens only once, lighting up the Nagual's fields like a lamp.

In the case of the Nagual who expresses the masculine, the emotional trauma causes the left-spinning, mental star tetrahedron to start spinning right, like the emotional one. The emotions totally override perception; and because they spin at different speeds, the cocoon cracks.

For the Nagual expressing the feminine, mental obsessions pull the right-spinning, emotional star tetrahedron left. As the mental and emotional star tetrahedrons now both spin counterclockwise at different speeds, her luminous cocoon cracks.

In the case of the three-pronged Nagual, the mental and emotional anguish each pull in two opposite directions with equal force. The tops of all three star tetrahedrons are then pulled counter-clockwise and the bottoms clockwise, ripping them apart and cracking the cocoon. Normally the field of light emitted by a person's spinning fields is the shape of a UFO (saucer-shaped). When the tops and bottoms spin independently, however, the three-pronged Nagual's fields resemble a large ball of light.

The goal for Naguals, as for all human beings, is to graduate beyond humanness to the God-kingdom, where a whole new evolutionary experience awaits. Here the Nagual's cocoon splits again. If he was a three-pronged Nagual before, the cocoon will now develop two cracks, which split into four prongs. The cocoon of a four-pronged Nagual develops only one crack which splits into 3 prongs. In both cases, the Naguals, no longer human, become seven-pronged Naguals, combining all skill sets and able to access all parts of reality.

The New Role of Naguals

Naguals no longer exist to lead others to freedom from illusion. At the end of July 2006 all illusion within the sphere of existence encompassed by the previous cycle had been solved. This doesn't mean that everything in all existence is known, but rather the allotted portion assigned to that specific cycle of life was completed. The previous cycle had fulfilled its destiny. It had solved all it undertook to solve.

The Nagual's new function is no longer focused on doing; now the focus is orientated on being, on getting to know that which is. The Nagual now walks a new path, assisting others in seeing their highest, most noble qualities,

He or she does this not only by mirroring it to another, seeing and appreciating it in another (we empower that which we focus on), but also by using the great many techniques at his or her disposal to dispel any barriers preventing expression of a noble trait. Laughter, fun, beauty, inspiration become the new tools. To stimulate the process, the Nagual must embody these traits and more. Now focusing entirely on the light, the Nagual dismisses all else as unreal, as that which no longer is.

I.6 Omnipresent Awareness

For eons, Toltec seers studied the various forms of awareness in the cosmos and found that all forms of awareness moved. Within the first days of August 2006, as we entered an entirely new creation, dramatic changes occurred in the very fabric of existence. For the first time since the Toltecs have been studying awareness, there is a new form of awareness, a static awareness permeating all life: Omnipresent Awareness.

What is Awareness?

There are three primary building blocks of reality: love, light and awareness. Love is the feminine aspect, light is the masculine and awareness, as the fusion of love and light, is neutral. The love and light form carrier waves for each other.

The cosmos utilizes imbalance to create the impetus for growth, since it is the nature of all things to strive to correct imbalance. The feminine now outweighs the masculine in a ratio of 80% feminine, 20% masculine. Since the feminine is stationary in this new creation, awareness, as a combination of the masculine and the stronger feminine, is also stationary.

Changes in the Previous Cycles

As we went through small changes in our lives or larger more dramatic ones, a pattern emerged—a map we could use to identify what stage of change we were in. Previously, change went through three distinct phases: transformation, transmutation and transfiguration.[4]

These three phases are no longer relevant to the process of change in our new creation. The new creation we entered in August 2006 ended the cycles and their stages as we knew them.

The cosmos, like man, is no longer subject to the three phases of change. It has now become free from cycles of death and rebirth. The 'inbreath and outbreath of God'[5] spoken about by mystics, has ceased. Death is overcome.

The Nature of the Cycles and Awareness

It is helpful to understand that awareness previously moved during now obsolete cycles. In the last cosmic cycle, awareness,

---

4. See The Anatomy of Change in *Journey to the Heart of God*.
5. See Stages of Man, 3.1

as trillions of spiraling rays, moved outwards from Source (that Infinite Being that gives birth to all life) forming a large arc. As the Infinite grew in knowledge through the experience of multiple beings, the arc grew larger. It created a large donut or tube toris that had to eventually return to Source. This created death.

In the last cycle which ended in August 2006, an additional movement occurred within the trillions of spiraling rays, prolonging life but not preventing death. Although the rays still formed a donut, centrifugal circular pulsations throughout the cosmos expanded it, delaying its return to Source. *(Figs. 4 and 5, The Movement of Awareness)*

Now the cosmos no longer needs cycles of death and rebirth. All previous spiraling rays of awareness have broken up into trillions and trillions of little pieces, spreading across the cosmos. The entire cosmos now has equal access to awareness; we don't need to search for enlightenment, it's all around and through us.

Having Full Access to Omnipresent Awareness

We cannot fully conceptualize the enormous gifts this accessibility to the Infinite's awareness brings. Growth no longer takes place through the old way of laboriously moving repeatedly through the three stages of change. Change can now come in an instant. After countless eons of striving to 'become', we now only need to 'align' and we are there!

Where exactly is 'there'? As enlightened as we want to be. The Infinite grows more aware with each fraction of a second, and so can we. Access to the Infinite's awareness is obtainable to the same degree as our ability to live in praise, love and gratitude.

The Movement of Awareness In Previous Cycles

Three movements exists in awareness to create the tube toris present where birth and rebirth cycles exist:

Original Awareness
Movement: It arcs
Originates: Within the Spirit Body
Polarity: Neutral

Inherent Awareness
Movement: A straight line
Originates: Within the Mental Body
Polarity: Masculine

Evolving Awareness
Movement: It spirals
Originates: Within the Physical Body
Polarity: Feminine

The three types of awareness create the tube torus of the Infinite and its Creation. It exists of trillions of arcing spirals propelling away from and returning to Source or originating point.

(Figure 4)

24

The Movement of Awareness In Previous Cycles

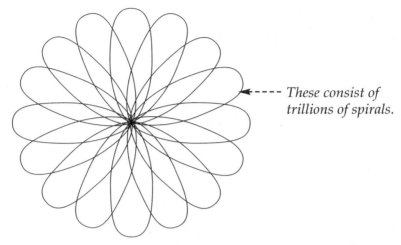

These consist of trillions of spirals.

The way awareness flowed through 9–18 cycles before this time.

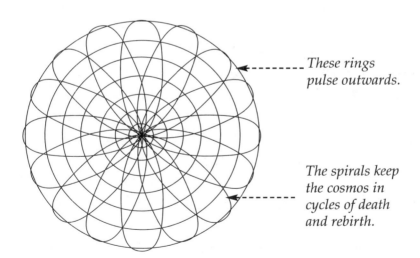

These rings pulse outwards.

The spirals keep the cosmos in cycles of death and rebirth.

The way awareness flowed through 1–9 cycles before this time.

(Figure 5)

The primary emotion at the core of the new creation is trust—the desire to surrender. Trust is the result of praise, love and gratitude; and in return, it engenders more love, praise and gratitude.

1.7 How to Create Through the Heart

The knowledge that we are creating our reality through thought and feeling is not new. At a deep, core level, lighworkers have been aware that they are responsible for their environment and their part in creating it. To change the victim mentality, large numbers of advanced starseeds have been birthing into humanity for three generations.

In order to study illusion in the previous cycle, we birthed situations that were flawed in that they were filled with illusion. We accomplished this by involving surface mind in the creation process. Its flawed perception birthed flawed creations.

The previous creation process went like this: thoughts fell into the reservoir of the heart and acted on the substance of things hoped for, which then formed as the circumstances of our environment. A clear way to understand this is that our most prevalent thought, coupled by our most sincere desire, became our life's circumstances. Intention externalized itself.

What is the substance of things hoped for and how did it respond to intent? We have mentioned that the way awareness was organized and moved during the previous cycle was in trillions of little rays that resembled spirals moving in great arcs, forming a huge tube toris that moved away from and towards Source as its point of origin.

We have also seen that the cosmos split itself the way a

Nagual's fields crack, as one cycle made way for another. This enabled it to hold more light.

Although the cosmos split on August 3, 2006, shattering **every** spiral of awareness into little bits, it also split before when we moved into the previous cycle. When that happened, **some** of the spirals were shattered into tiny fragments, filling the spaces between the spirals.

These infinitesimal rays, or spirals, of awareness moved (something they no longer do), pummeling everything and penetrating deeply into even the densest matter. They responded to thoughts and feelings by rolling themselves into little balls and forming the atoms necessary to materialize our circumstances. In other words, thoughts plus feelings clustered awareness into form.

Now, it is in the emptiness of mind and through the heart that perfection (that which reflects the true nature of the Infinite's being), or absolute truth, is born.

Every being that has earned the right to be in the new creation is a reflection of truth and light. Those who reflected or created illusion have ceased to be. They have been either made obsolete by the new purpose of life, which is to reflect absolute truth; or they re-formed into pristine purity, reflecting and creating that which is, rather than that which is not.

Now that mind, with its ability to be deceived, no longer plays a crucial part in creating, what then will cluster the now very available awareness into form? It is love, praise and gratitude.

Love, praise and gratitude are attitudes. An attitude[6] is a mindset (a way of perceiving life) coupled with emotion. It is an interaction of light and frequency.

So also is awareness. Awareness forms through the fusion of frequency and light into carrier waves for each other, marrying two primary elements of creation. If a little ray of awareness could be cut to reveal a cross-section, it would resemble a wobbly cross, with frequency as the horizontal wave merged with the vertical wave of light.

The new laws of existence decree that with light and frequency opposites now attract. Awareness has become passive in that it no longer moves, and is therefore negatively charged. The three ascension attitudes of love, praise and gratitude are expansive and proactive, therefore positively charged.

Wherever love, praise and gratitude exist, awareness will rush into that area of their influence. Their strength dictates the size of the creation we can birth. The little rays of awareness roll upon themselves, forming atoms (matter). Creation of the true and beautiful in this way takes place through the heart.

1.8 Love, Praise and Gratitude

The attitudes of love, praise, and gratitude are representative of the trinity found throughout the matrix of existence. They crown a sanctified life in glory and carry man to immortality and ascension awaiting beyond his present horizon.

Love

Emerson wrote:

> *"Alas! I know not why... each man sees over his own*
> *experience a certain stain of error, whilst that of other*
> *men looks fair and ideal."*

6. Love can also be an element or building block of creation as represented by the direction of Below. It can be an emotion when based on the desire to include. Our language doesn't have adequate wording to differentiate its various natures.

The word love is bandied about; it streams from pulpits, across restaurant tables, in flowery cards of all descriptions. The fact is that very few philosophers have shed much light on how the love we feel in romance and the love for God and Creation can be reconciled. There is an abundance of literature which extols romantic love; yet many spiritual writings dismiss it as an unworthy reflection of infinite love.

Because romantic love is the most intoxicating feeling most humans will ever have (called by philosophers 'the enchantment of human life'), it has been compounded by feelings of guilt that such intense love should instead have been given to God. In the lives of most, no love will ever again compare to the heady, runaway, romantic emotion of youth. In this quandary, we found ourselves lacking in devotion; and so tried to love God with all the fervor we could muster. For many, this was a nebulous and undefined concept, often creating religious fanatics who, failing in their feelings, tried to compensate through their actions.

The very turbulence of our romantic love carves out of our souls the hollows that will hold a greater love. Through love for a father, a mother, a child, a lover, etc., our love grows to include all people.

Intense romantic love awakens within us the ability to love others more deeply; but it also awakens so much more. The depth an artist brings to art likewise stems from passion inspired by love. Eventually, not only that which we create but that which we are, gets honed and shaped into a maturity that is lacking in those who have never truly loved another.

We learn through our earthly loves how to surrender to something greater, that one day we may merge with our own higher identity. We find through love's muse the poet within us, the spontaneity of the inner child. We know what it is like to follow our hearts and abandon reason. Love mellows us and reduces our resistance to life and as we grow older; what we forfeit in intensity we gain in inclusiveness.

The heart cannot fully love while there is an internal dialog, though one can only know that retrospectively. As the mind silences, the heart bursts open with an all-encompassing melting tenderness for all life. Divine love takes its place upon the throne of the heart.

Praise

As a child, I had a fear of heights. When on the high rides of the carnival or perched in our mulberry tree, I found that I could overcome my fear by focusing on the far horizon. By slightly altering the focus of my eyes, the dizzy heights became friendlier.

Praise is an attitude that focuses on the distant vistas and allows itself to enjoy the breathtaking view. It acknowledges that there is an unpaid bill, but focuses instead on the nurturing and abundant supply that flows to one who trusts in it.

Praise is an attitude of thoughts raised heavenward, nowhere better illustrated than the story of Christ walking on the water as told in the New Testament. He did not focus on the stormy seas, but steadfastly kept his focus on indwelling life rather than form. The disciple Peter, who wished to walk on the water also, saw the billowing waves and the high winds and sank. The master had to reach forth his hand and save him. Christ lived in a state of praise, but Peter did not.

As an ascension attitude, praise needs to be tempered by experience. It is not enough to withdraw from life to spend our days singing songs of praise to God. Our highest purpose in being here is to explore the known.

There is no redundancy in the cosmos. If there is a beggar in the street, there is also the need for him to be there. It could be that a great master has undertaken to play this role, to give us the opportunity for compassionate understanding. Whatever the reason may be, there will be ample cause for praise if we change our focus from appearances to indwelling life.

Praise fills the cells with light and our footsteps become a blessing to the earth. All life we touch responds with increased growth to such a life affirming frequency. Filled with praise we also fill with increased light and life force.

Gratitude

If true happiness lies in being happy with what we have, rather than being happy when we get what we want, gratitude is the key to happiness. It helps us value the little joys of the moment rather than wait for the large windfalls, and in doing so we learn to appreciate life.

Life consists of the small treasures like the quiet oasis of the undisturbed moment with a cup of tea that allows us to return to the inner world of contemplation. We can turn the weary tread of drudgery into a lightened gait with gratitude. The cherishing warmth of a favorite quilt on a dark, rain drenched night; the moment of feeling the coming of spring in the air; the rosy cheeked pleasure of rocking a little child to sleep, eyelids weighted by the adventures of her day; all these treasured moments through awareness become ample reason for a heart to brim with gratitude.

Not only does gratitude bless us with joy, but also with increase. One of the most concealed laws of supply is that gratitude opens the floodgates of heaven, increasing anything it focuses on. Would we wish to increase our health, our abundance, and our abilities? Then the place to begin is in grateful acknowledgement of whatever we already have. Let us focus in appreciation and joy on how much it means to have it. With each dollar we spend with sincere, heartfelt gratitude, many more will find their way into our pocket.

Like the other ascension attitudes, gratitude is life affirming to all whom it contacts. Indigenous peoples have always known that nature responds favorably to gratitude; that species thrive and evolve under the grateful recognition of man. Gratitude sanctifies not only the giver, but also the recipient.

Inclusiveness demands that gratitude must not deem one as worthy and another as not; but like the sun or the life giving rain, gratitude must shed its radiance on pain and pleasure alike. It takes in-depth insight to probe behind the appearances and extract the eternal truth that Mother sends nothing but goodness.

1.9 Why Time is Standing Still

Time is the movement of awareness. Until now, all awareness moved because its most dominant component, emotion (the feminine), moved.

In the new creation, the feminine emotion is stationary. It holds the matrix of existence by remaining in twelve concentric stationary rings, while the masculine (light) moves. Therefore the dominant component of awareness (again the feminine) doesn't move; and time, as the movement of awareness, doesn't exist.

Linear time, as we once knew it, does not exist. It collapsed before the end of the last cycle. The symbol I was given is a double pointed crystal collapsing into the middle, forming a diamond. This means the last moment and the next are both contained in this moment.

In the illusion of linear time, if we had to draw on past experiences, we could re-experience past moments by accessing them in this moment, through memory. The non-existence of time as movement is a different matter. The moments are no longer disconnected from one another in a linear timeline, rather they all exist in the present moment.

Where the effects of this difference will be felt most profoundly is in memory. Unless we cling to the illusion of time, it will simply be as though the last moment never existed; as though we have no memory whatsoever. It will be difficult to remember even what we said a few minutes ago. Will this be inconvenient and create problems for us? Only if we try to live in the old way.

The complexity of the relationship between time and space determines density, directly affecting the density of the electro-magnetic fields that hold memory. Where there is no time and space there is no density, causing the electro-magnetic fields to collapse and memory to disappear.

We used to define 'space' as the gridwork or matrix of existence. In the new creation, the grids and matrix are determined by the seven directions and the 12 rings of emotion.

In past cycles, 'space' had a limit; and cycles of existence played out within those limits. In the new creation, 'space' by the old definition of a non-flexible matrix, doesn't exist. The rings of emotion do provide a boundary within which the sixteen rays of light bounce, but the boundaries are flexible.

The light beams move through and within the rings of emotion in a very specific dance and, although there are no angles and joints, they cross each other without touching. At the culmination of each dance, they combine to form two overlapping circles, forming a vesica pisces and expanding the boundaries formed by the rings of emotion. In this way perception yields expanded emotion.

As we live the emotions, allowing them to grow greater and greater by pulsing their masculine and feminine aspects, the rings themselves expand. The rings of emotion are frequency bands. In the new creation, with frequency and light, like repels like. The distance between the rings must be maintained by their force that pushes them apart.

What this means in application, is that even if only one set of emotions is fully lived and its specific ring expands, the other emotions will expand likewise.

As we live and expand the emotions, their rings increase in diameter. Space, in other words, has become fluid. The womb of this new creation provides increased space in which perception or light can dance. In this way, increased emotion also increases perception.

Living the New Way

With no memory and no density to hold us back, there is no time lapse necessary in which to grow or become. All we can be is available to us right now. The determining factor is how fully we can live with the attitudes of love, praise and gratitude.

- If we stay in the place of complete silence of the mind, we will speak automatically without thought. We say the right thing and do the right thing (the highest choice) at the correct moment.

- Where memory used to be kept in mind, there will now be effortless knowing—which is what genius consists of. There will be an empty stage for light to dance. The key is to not second-guess ourselves, as effortless knowing supersedes reason.

- Before, we relied on memory to determine patterns; to determine, for instance, if the good outweighed the bad in a relationship. Because patterns are no longer held, due to the collapsing of electro-magnetic fields, and because massive change can now occur in an instant, we don't need memory.

How do we know whether to keep a relationship? We don't need to know. At the right moment, when the energies are incompatible enough, they will automatically repel each other. All we have to do is surrender, which is trust. That which is compatible will then be drawn in. Strife and struggle have yielded to peace.

1.10 The Language of the Holy Mother

(See Fig. 6, The Language of the Holy Mother)

Sentences and Phrases:

1. Aushbava heresh sishisim (Come here)
2. Va-aal vi-ish paru-es (Do it again)
3. Kre-eshna sa-ul varavaa (It is beautiful everywhere)
4. Pranuvaa sanuvesh vilsh-savu bravispa (We are with you

The Language of the Holy Mother

Magic is in the moment (vursh venestu parneshtu)

Great things await. (Iuvishpa niutrim sarem)

Let the fun begin. (Ruftravasbi iulem)

Please take me with you. (Nun brash barnut pareshvi)

(Figure 6)

when you think of us)

5. Aasushava pre-unan aruva bareesh (We come to open the gate.) Note that "come" in this sense is not the same word used for "come here".

6. Oonee/varunish heshpiu tra barin (Everyone is dancing with joy)

7. Belesh bri anur bra vershpi iulan (Take away the frown from your face)

8. Nen hursh avervi tranuk averva? (When comes the moment of laughing?) Note: there is no word for time.

9. Nun brash barnut pareshvi (Please take us with you)

10. Vursh venestu parneshtu (Magic is the moment)

11. Iuvishpa niutrim sarem (Great things await)

12. Ruftravasbi iulem (Let the fun begin)

13. Verluash verurlabaa mi urla set viunish (Be prepared for the fulfillment of your dreams)

14. Be-ulahesh parve mi-ur ville Starva (Speak to us through these sacred words)

15. Truaveshviesh aluvispaha maurnanuhe. (Welcome to the fullness of our being)
Telech nusva rura vesbi (Through love are we connected)

16. Erluech spauhura vavish menuba. (Find the new song that you sing)

17. Me-uhu vaubaresh ka-ur-tum (Our new dance is a joyous one)

18. Pelech parve uru-uhush vaspa pe-uravesh ple-ura. (Together let us create wonderous moments)

20. Vala veshpa uvi kle-u vishpi ula usbeuf pra-uva. (You are invited into the loving embrace of our arms)

21. Perenuesh krava susibreve truache. (In great mercy you are renewed)
22. Pleshpaa vu skaura versebia nunuhesh. (Allow your shouders to feel lightness)
23. Verunachva ulusetvaabi manuresh. (All suffering is in this moment redeemed)
24. Keleustraha virsabaluf bra uvraha. (You dwell in us and are ours)
25. Keleshpruanesh te le-usbaru (Call and we shall hear)

(Figs. 7, 8, 9, The Alphabet of the Holy Mother)

I.II How the New Cosmos was Created

Earthly gods have traditionally not played a major part in the creation process; but now they do. Some were present at the creation of the new cosmos, which took place in the first few days of August, 2006.

Mother of All (the Goddess of Creation) had created a womb within her Being (this is basically what a cosmos is) in which Creation was to form. Twelve goddesses then embodied the twelve emotional or frequency bands; and through them, the rest of creation was formed. The formation took place from the inside out, with the trust/love sphere forming first; the peace/inspiration sphere second, and so on.

(Figs. 10, 11, 12 How the Cosmos Formed)

These spheres are stationary, forming the matrix of Creation. Whereas previously the matrix was masculine, being comprised of stationary light, the new creation has a feminine matrix comprised of frequency.

With a tone, a line of white light appeared along the edge of

Alphabet of The Holy Mother

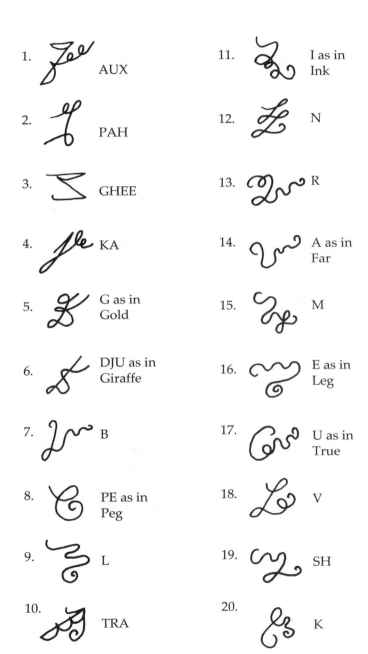

1. AUX

2. PAH

3. GHEE

4. KA

5. G as in Gold

6. DJU as in Giraffe

7. B

8. PE as in Peg

9. L

10. TRA

11. I as in Ink

12. N

13. R

14. A as in Far

15. M

16. E as in Leg

17. U as in True

18. V

19. SH

20. K

(Figure 7)

39

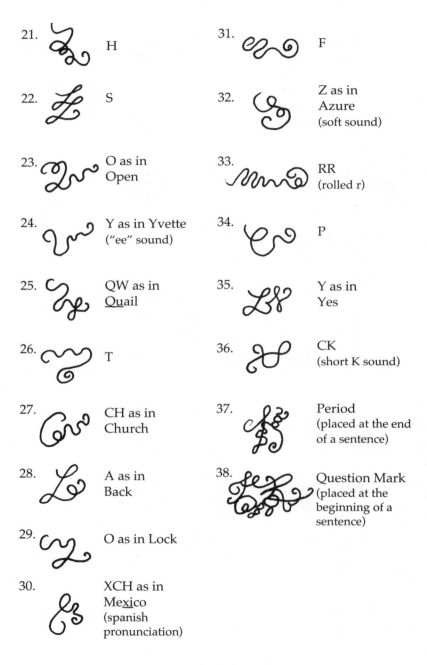

21. H

22. S

23. O as in Open

24. Y as in Yvette ("ee" sound)

25. QW as in Quail

26. T

27. CH as in Church

28. A as in Back

29. O as in Lock

30. XCH as in Mexico (spanish pronunciation)

31. F

32. Z as in Azure (soft sound)

33. RR (rolled r)

34. P

35. Y as in Yes

36. CK (short K sound)

37. Period (placed at the end of a sentence)

38. Question Mark (placed at the beginning of a sentence)

(Figure 8)

Additional Letters of Other Languages—
Used in the Holy Mothers Language

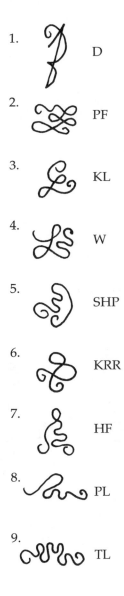

1. D

2. PF

3. KL

4. W

5. SHP

6. KRR

7. HF

8. PL

9. TL

(Figure 9)

How the Cosmos Formed

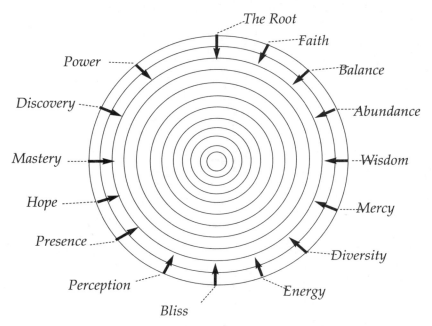

Initially only 15 Rays form through tones.

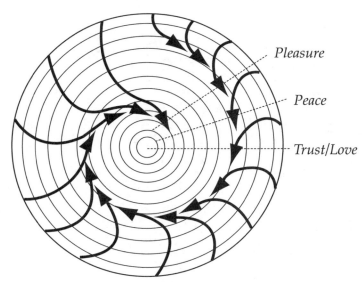

The 15 Rays take shape at the edge of the cosmic womb but bend in a clockwise direction, becoming one as they enter sphere of Trust.

(Figure 10)

Continued: How the Cosmos Formed

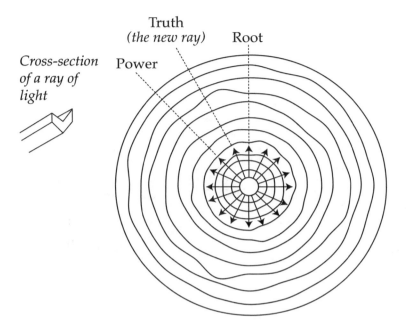

Center sphere is spinning and shoots out 16 Rays.
The new 16th ray of truth is born.

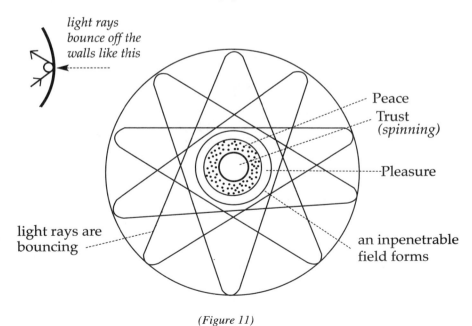

(Figure 11)

Continued: How the Cosmos Formed

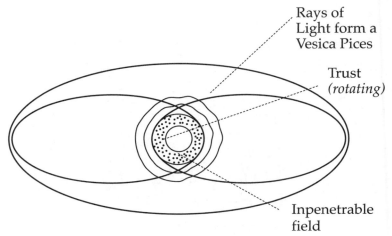

The twelve rings are stretched into an oval.

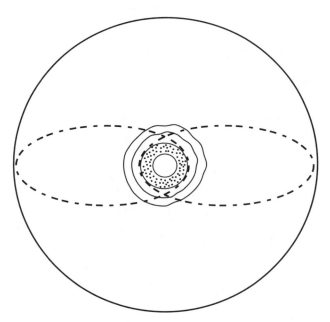

The rings enlarge to form perfect spheres again. Expansion results.

(Figure 12)

the womb. In succession, each with a specific tone, 15 colors of light appeared. As they grew, they started moving clockwise, flowing into each other in a spiral form. *(Fig. 13, How Light and Emotion Interact in the New Creation)* At the 15th ray, which is power, they entered the center sphere of trust/love in a blinding burst of white light.

At the moment of entry, the middle sphere of trust started spinning. As it reached a specific velocity, not 15, but 16 rays of light shot out. A 16th pink ray had been born: the ray of absolute truth. *(Fig. 14, Sixteen Rays of Light Moving in the Cosmos)* The light rays are Y shaped if seen in cross-section, and in this new creation, they move in a specific dance through the cosmos.

The spinning of the sphere of trust/love in the center formed a field just on the outer edge of the stationary 3rd sphere of Pleasure/Creativity, impenetrable to the re-entry of the light rays. They therefore bounce off this field during the dance they do.

The dance of the 16 rays traces all our Plutonic solids' shapes, but without angles, as the illusion of their having angles and joints was just part of our lack of perception in the dense portions of the previous cycle. Although there were differences from the shapes and creational sequences of this creation, cosmic geometry has never had angles and joints in any cycle.

When the dance of the rays is at its most expansive, they force the womb of Creation into an oval, creating a vesica pisces. Because the frequency bands are all the same type of frequency, they repel each other. In order to maintain their equidistance, the bands have to now expand to correct the areas where they were drawn too close together as they were pulled

How Light and Emotion Interact in the New Creation

When Emotion Yields Perception

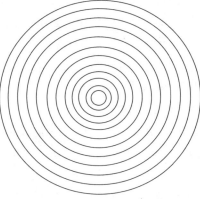

Each ring, representing a pair of emotions, keeps a specific distance from the others because like frequencies repel.

If one of the emotions, in this instance, TRUST (the middle ring) expands, as with any other ring, it comes to close to the next ring.

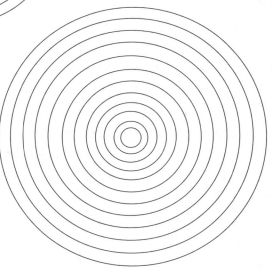

The rings push outward to adjust the space. The womb in which light can bounce is now bigger. Emotion has yielded increased perception.

(Figure 13)

Sixteen Rays of Light Moving in the Cosmos

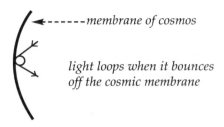

------- *membrane of cosmos*

light loops when it bounces off the cosmic membrane

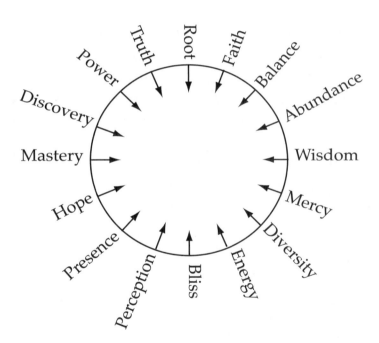

The sixteen rays of light, representing certain attributes, bounce of the border of the cosmos. In the new cosmic cycle, light moves and emotional frequency bands and awareness are static.

(Figure 14)

into an oval. They reform into a larger sphere; enlarging the womb of Creation. *(Fig. 15, How Light and Emotion Interact in this Cycle)*

Growth in the previous cycle occurred through incorporating the previous cosmic spaces or wombs through which we had descended multiple times. The new creation is a "blank canvas" and has never been lived before. Growth therefore takes on a whole new meaning. It is now expansion versus (formerly) becoming.

There is another huge difference pertaining to the life of an individual. Although we have always affected the whole by our actions, we can now make an even bigger difference. If we embody one of the emotional bands more fully than has ever been done before, we can expand that particular emotional sphere.

The other bands must then also expand to keep their equi-distance. In this way, we can more fully become that which Mother is; we can work with her as co-creators of the cosmic expansion; we can promote cosmic growth.

I.12 How to Create Through The Heart

In the new creation, we create only through the heart; no longer will chaotic thoughts manifest chaotic circumstances. We can love only that which we can recognize; and we can recognize only what is inside ourselves. We are, in essence, re-creating our most beautiful or loveable parts.

Let us say we want to pull into actuality a magnificent home for ourselves. We would find everything we want to create outside of ourselves, within, entering fully into it emotionally. We

How Light and Emotion Interact in this Cycle
When Perception Yields Emotion

The Light rays follow a specific dance

A ray of light bounces off the walls of the womb of the new cycle of creation. There are no cycles and no joints.

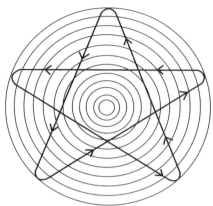

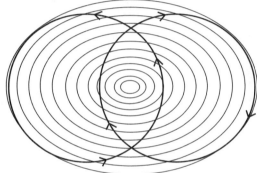

At the end of each dance they form a Vesica Pisces

The movement of perception, or light enlarges the emotional rings to an oval.

The emotional or frequency rings correct the distance between them forming a larger womb than before. Perception has enhanced emotion.

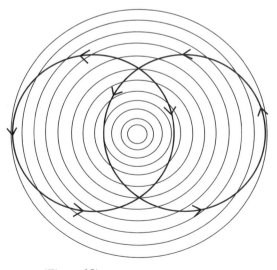

(Figure 15)

would feel the deep contentment of the warmth of our bed as the rain falls on the roof; the cushioned feel of deeply cherished rugs beneath our feet. We would delight in the dawn's first light falling on a beautiful painting; and the inspiration of vaulted ceilings and magnificent architecture.

Deeply feel these emotions. Imagine the emotions filling a sphere around you the size of the house you want. Take as long as it needs to fill the sphere with emotion. Stay in your feelings.

Then imagine that you are drawing a line from the sphere of emotion you are in, to where you want your house to be. In the same size sphere, see your emotions externalize the house you had felt, into form. In this way, you can also give others the beautiful attributes you have. But you know that light-workers have been giving and giving for millennia. It is time for the flow to reverse; to bring the balance of receptivity to the ages of generosity. In other words, it's time for us to dream in what we would love to receive.

1.13 Detoxifying: A Natural Result of the New Polarity

In the previous cycle where opposite energies attracted, light-workers not only attracted people of distorted, opposite energies, but they also attracted toxicity in all forms. Air- and food-borne toxins have a lower energy and were likewise attracted by light-workers. Lightworkers were also apt to battle chemical and other toxicities by eating pure foods; and because like energies repelled, a compounding problem reared its head: mal-absorption. From mal-absorption and toxicity, increased numbers of attention deficit children were born. We were locked into a very unhealthy cycle in that the better we ate and the purer our energy became, the more susceptible we became to the toxins we inevitably encountered.

This dynamic no longer applies. Now that similar energies attract and opposites repel, toxins will no longer be absorbed, but excreted. In fact the stronger the light filled energies, the more dramatic the elimination.

Likewise, the need for tolerance of dysfunctionality in our environment will be dramatically less. Compassion used to mean tolerance of that which we are not, but now it means separating ourselves from it.

The beautiful gift of this new creation is that everything conspires to support the light-worker into flourishing. Growth through support truly replaces growth through opposition.

1.14 Density as an Energy Source

Previously, negativity could be a mirror of something within us; but every being has been re-created into that which is light- and love-filled, that which is what the Infinite Mother is. We therefore know that we are not the negativity; that it represents the clinging to obsolete patterns. Negativity does not help us fulfill the purpose of this creation, to explore the true nature of our being. There is therefore no reason we need to engage or explore the negativity of others. Instead, we use our stomachs to digest anything negative directed at us.

The light-workers on earth are becoming 100% light.[7] Some are finding they no longer need to eat. However, a being that isn't using his stomach to turn food into energy, can still use it

7. Belvaspata's level 2 initiation symbols facilitate this.

to turn the negativity of others into an energy source.

As a negative emotion is directed at you, simply see it drawn to and entering the stomach. Then see it churn around and around, becoming lighter and lighter until it turns to a light that spreads through the body.

Anger and rage are the hardest to digest and could feel like a lump in the stomach for days. Deep 'stomach' breaths that move the stomach in and out help, in conjunction with intention and visualization. Remember don't blow the density out with your breaths—it has become your 'food', your energy supply.

Energy can be increased by 40% from lower level 'love' that is directed at one. The love of another, when tainted with lust, agenda and control cannot be received through the heart; it leaves an energetic black mark on the heart. But received into the stomach, it is turned into increased energy. Increased energy increases consciousness, effortlessly and easily.

1.15 Conversation with Thoth 16th September 2006

Q. I am so very glad to have received the insights on how to thrive on others' density. One can turn the lower choices of others into advantage—lemons into lemonade. This information has become available at this time because it's very pertinent right now, isn't it?

A. Yes it is. Don't you want to know the rest? Why have you had so many irritating individuals around you, at train stations, airports, and hotel check-in desks?

Q. I've been trying to understand it. I ….

A. That's part of the problem.

Q. What is?

A. It sticks in your mind and makes a black mark.

Q. But I only allow something to stick in my mind when I know there's something I'm not seeing..?

A.That's the old way.

Q. And in addition, isn't this cycle a period where we can repel? In fact, as the new form of compassion, aren't we <u>supposed</u> to repel that which isn't harmonious with our energy?

A.Yes.

Q. Then why the black mark?

A.Because you allow it to stick in your head; to bother you.

Q. Ahaa! I should treat these "unpleasant little daily shocks" of others' inability to 'see', just as I did the huge big shocks that happened at the end of the last cycle when the horrible treachery was uncovered?

A. Go on...

Q. I stayed in absolute emptiness, because the shock of it would've drained my energy, lowering my consciousness. Are you saying that, in the emptiness of thought, any areas where action is needed will reveal themselves?

A. And the repelling will take place at the appropriate time and place.

Q.It once more comes down to trusting the perfection of the big picture?

A. It definitely does!

1.16 Supported Growth vs. Inertia

Toltec seers encountered the principle of inertia throughout the cosmos as they traveled through the loops and wormholes of time and space. This principle has now disappeared—an occurrence of great importance—making it even easier to reach and maintain our maximum potential at all times.

In essence, inertia meant that in order to maintain levels of growth, constant amounts of energy were needed to support that level. For this reason I have previously stressed that life was a journey, not a camp. One was either moving forward or sliding backwards; never standing still.

The only way to maintain the status quo was to work at it. To be able to grow beyond it, took an additional amount of work. Growth therefore had not been an easy matter—one had to be relentless. Any concept of easing up on growth produced a one step forward, two steps backward routine. But since growth came through hardship and opposition, the journey of growth as a constant, became too grueling for most.

This principle of inertia found in all cosmoses within the previous cycle resulted from a deliberate plan by the primary male god of that cycle in order to maintain his patriarchal rule. His plan was to force every ascension at the top of that cycle, back into descension. To accomplish this, he injured or drained the goddesses associated with time and the movement of time (found in the east). As we have stated, in the previous cycles awareness moved. This movement created time, and also pressured perception into expansion. The more rapid the movement of time, the more rapid the growth. By tampering with the goddesses of time, he slowed time's movement, which produced the following results:

• Slower expansion of perception and hence slower growth;

- The creation of linear time—something that was never meant to be;
- Linear time enabled light-repressors to be able to move back and forth through time, hindering light-promoters and tampering with beneficial outcomes;
- Linear time produced density, the obscuring of light;
- The relationship between cause and effect became hidden as density delayed effects. When we could not clearly see the results of an action, we tended to not take responsibility for our choices, and could also feel victimized—which was keeping us in an undeveloped, infantile state;
- He caused the principle of inertia by the unresolved density of the former multiple ascension/descension cycles. Think of it as trying to get up a hill after accumulating heavy baggage in the back of a truck. In slowing the speed of growth by slowing the movement of time, inertia developed; and he prevented the cosmos from having the momentum to break through into the next cycle. We were like the truck, heavily laden, trying to get up the hill without enough speed. It took all the gas we had just to stay on one spot without even managing to make it to the top and over.

In the new creation, there is no time and there is no density or debris from previous experience. Also, there's no illusion (except that which can be described as obsolete patterns some may cling to) or unresolved pieces. We can have all awareness now through the ascension attitudes—we don't have a linear 'road up the mountain.' We therefore can't backslide either.

Awareness gained is sustained by the new laws:

1. Awareness does not move, except when it is pulled towards a source of love, praise, and gratitude—the three aspects of

what forms the positive portion of awareness.

2. Once pulled towards the source (you), it is going to stay there, since nothing other than these attitudes is going to cause it to move.

3. So even if for some reason you temporarily cease to feel those attitudes, the awareness still remains with you.

After delving into that which was unreal, we have entered into that which is real, namely Mother's Being. We cannot backslide because she supports our growth. Growth is now a very joyful process; and we can grow and expand at any pace we choose.

1.17 The Ascent of Man

Within the cosmic cycles we have just completed, our relationship to the gods in the god kingdoms was not dissimilar to our relationship to our earthly governments. We were an exploitable resource to them, kept uninformed, disempowered and dependent. The payoff was supposed to be that they would 'take care' of us, which they did not do.

Just how much they abused the trust we put in their leadership, did not come to light until the treachery within these kingdoms was exposed at the end of the previous cycle. But with foresight that exceeded that of most others, one of those who had made it into the god kingdom, the Christ, prophesied of these times.

He said the first would be last and the last would be first, that the meek would inherit the earth. A great purging did indeed happen. Based on the degree to which each being had become life-enhancing and 'meek' or harmless, their worthiness was assessed as to whether or not they had earned 'eternal life' (Christ frequently referred to this) in the new creation.

Previously material life was created from the higher realms, making us feel very much as a child in relation to its parents. But something extraordinary has happened: the ascent of man. Only one god has survived from the old hierarchy, namely Thoth; and there is no longer a hierarchy. There is Leadership, which is determined by who has the most love, praise and gratitude. In this new leadership, man plays a vital role.

More and more ascended masters predominant not only in earthly realms, but also to a lesser extent in other star systems, are entering the god kingdom. This means they are no longer human. These gods of material life are playing a huge role in the creation of the cosmos and its creatures.

On the 17th August 2006, earthly gods participated in an event, too holy for words in a book to convey, to re-create life in the new cosmos. The gods of the directions, goddesses of the emotions, gods and goddesses of light (also known as the gods and goddesses of Amenti) and other primary gods and goddesses were all called.[8] *(Figs. 16–19, Sigils for Further Gods & Goddesses) (Figs. 20, 21, Goddesses of the Twelve Rings of Emotion) (Figs. 22–27, Sigils of the Gods & Goddesses of Amenti)*

The significance of this is that we have become the co-creators with Mother; no longer the child, but the parent. Directions and flow have reversed. The first have become last and the last have become first—a fitting reward for those in the cosmos who have suffered the most that all may grow.

8. See Realms of the God-Kingdoms in *Mysteries of the Hidden Realms.*

Sigils for Further Gods and Goddesses

1. The God of Nature

2. The Goddess of the Devas

3. The Goddess of Deliverance

4. The Goddess of Nurturing

5. The Goddess of Enjoyment

6. The Goddess of Dispelling Illusions

(Figure 16)

Continued: Sigils for Further Gods and Goddesses

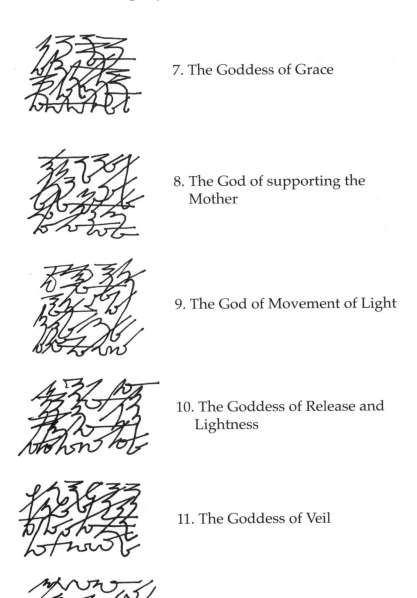

7. The Goddess of Grace

8. The God of supporting the Mother

9. The God of Movement of Light

10. The Goddess of Release and Lightness

11. The Goddess of Veil

12. The Goddess of Transmutation

(Figure 17)

Continued: Sigils for Further Gods and Goddesses

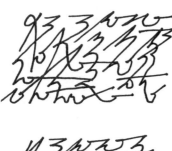 13. The Goddess of Compassion

 14. The Goddess of Prosperity

 15. The Goddess of Transfiguration

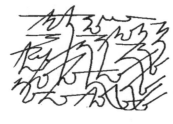 16. The Goddess of Transformation

 17. The God of Light

(Figure 19)

Twelve Rings of Emotion Goddesses

 1. The Goddess of Trust/Love

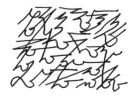 2. The Goddess of
Peace/Inspiration

 3. The Goddess of
Pleasure/Creativity

 4. The Goddess of
Acknowledgement/Empathy

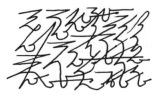 5. The Goddess of
Receptivity/Generosity

 6. The Goddess of
Beauty/Encouragement

(Figure 20)

Continued: Twelve Rings of Emotion Goddesses

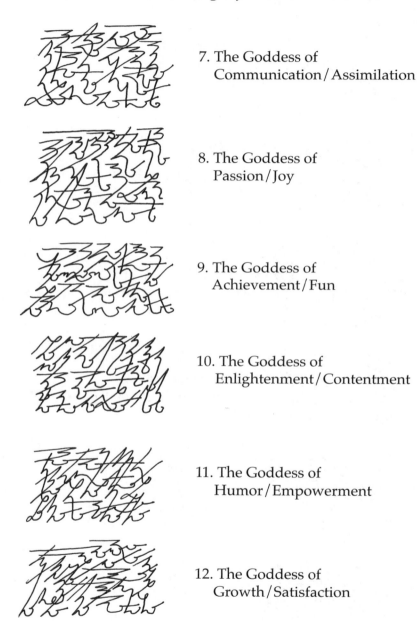

7. The Goddess of
   Communication/Assimilation

8. The Goddess of
   Passion/Joy

9. The Goddess of
   Achievement/Fun

10. The Goddess of
    Enlightenment/Contentment

11. The Goddess of
    Humor/Empowerment

12. The Goddess of
    Growth/Satisfaction

*These Goddesses are given in the order the rings formed from
the inner to the outer spheres.*

(Figure 21)

Sigils of the Gods and Goddesses of Amenti

Before the 3rd October, 2006

 1. The Root–The Mother of Creation

 2. The Goddess of Faith

 3. The Goddess of Balance

 4. The Goddess of Abundance

 5. The God of Wisdom

(Figure 22)

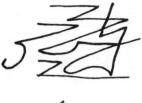
6. The Goddess of Mercy

7. The Goddess of Diversity

8. The God of Energy

9. The Goddess of Bliss

10. The God of Perception

(Figure 22)

Continued: Sigils of the Gods and Goddesses of Amenti

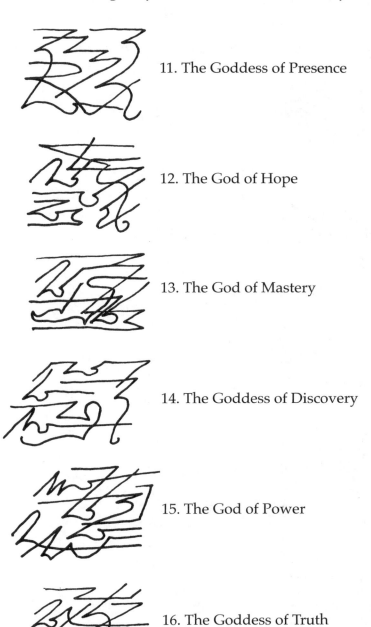

11. The Goddess of Presence

12. The God of Hope

13. The God of Mastery

14. The Goddess of Discovery

15. The God of Power

16. The Goddess of Truth

(Figure 23)

Sigils for the 16 New Gods and Goddesses of Amenti

After the cosmos increased in frequency on the 3rd October, 2006

 1. The Goddess of the Root of Light (Creator Goddess)

 2. The Goddess of Faith

 3. The Goddess of Balance

 4. The Goddess of Abundance

 5. The God of Wisdom

(Figure 25)

6. The Goddess of Presence

7. The God of Hope

8. The God of Mastery

9. The Goddess of Bliss

10. The Goddess of Perception

(Figure 26)

Continued: Sigils of 16 New Gods and Goddesses of Amenti

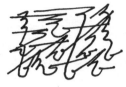 11. The Goddess of Mercy

 12. The Goddess of Diversity

 13. The Goddess of Energy

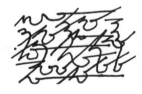 14. The Goddess of Discovery

 15. The God of Power

 16. The God of Truth

(Figure 27)

I.18 The Fulfillment of the Prophecies of Christ

Christ (one of only 9 Ascended Masters who, prior to August 2005, moved from the human kingdom into the God-Kingdom[9]) was able to perceive the closing of the cycle that took place at the end of July 2006. Many of his prophecies, including the ones he gave to John at Patmos that became the Book of Revelations, could really not be properly understood until then.

The lack of comprehension had been further aggravated by the removal of any and all references to the primary deity as a Goddess. Any hint of the sacred feminine had been eliminated by early scribes and by the intervention of the primary male god who sought to sway the majority at the top of the last cycle of creation into accepting him as the only Infinite. Because of the critical role of humanity as the archetype for the cosmos, swaying them to believe only in a male deity was a necessary strategic move. Male rule would bring about another descension into illusion.

The male god did manage to sway the majority. It was foreseen that he would influence one third, described in <u>Rev. 8:12.</u> "*...a third of the sun was struck, a third of the moon, and a third of the stars, so that a third of them were darkened. A third of the day did not shine, and likewise the night.*" In fact, *the god* swayed <u>two-thirds</u>.

We have already mentioned in our audio lectures and books that the New Jerusalem (see Revelations Ch. 21) is being prepared to house the Eternal Mother on earth. Be aware that the references to the 'great God', etc., need to read 'the great Goddess'. We have also explained in the section on The Realms of Arulu in *Secrets of the Hidden Realms* that as the earth start-

9. See Realms of the God-Kingdoms in *Mysteries of the Hidden Realms*.

ed its ascension, shown on our calendar as February, '05, it moved the heavens in a way that *"The sky receded as a scroll when it is rolled up."* Rev. 6:14. This resulted in a *"...new heaven and a new earth,"* Rev. 21:1, a fact that has been hidden from man (to avoid instilling terror) by the imposition of a hologram that still shows the heavens as they were.

The most holy and magnificent event of the Eternal Mother's coronation in the Halls of Amenti on earth fulfilled the prophecy that says *"...now a great sign (that) appeared in the heaven, a woman clothed with the sun, with the moon under her feet and on her head a garland of twelve stars."* Rev. 12:1. The rebellion of the *"great, fiery red dragon"*[10] described in verse 3 was also an event that was dealt with in 2005.

Even though the plagues, afflictions, earth changes and the war in heaven that were planned by the red dragon have been circumvented, much of Revelations and portions of the four gospels tell of the close of the old cycle. They are also quite clear about the ushering in of the new creation and the reign of the Mother Goddess on earth. The following prophecies have now taken on a whole new meaning.

1. The Great Judgment

> *"Most assuredly I say to you, he who believes in Her*[11]
> *who sent me has everlasting life and shall not come*
> *into judgment, but has passed from death into life.*
> *Do not marvel at this, for the hour is coming in which*
> *all who are in the graves will hear Her voice...*

10. Fully described in sections, The Old Dragon Insults Mother, and The Changing of an Ancient Dynasty, *Secrets of the Hidden Realms*.

11. Scripture will reflect the corrected feminine version.

*...and come forth—those who have done good, to the
resurrection of life, and those who have done evil, to
the resurrection of condemnation."* <u>John 5:24, 28, 29</u>
*Because you have kept my command to persevere, I also
will keep you from the hour of trial which shall come
upon the whole world, to test who dwell on earth."*
<u>Rev. 3:10</u>

At the end of July 2006, at the close of the cycle that had lasted for trillions of years, a great judgment occurred. More than two-thirds of the cosmos had turned against Mother. Humans were spared who did so without awareness of their actions. This is because they weren't conscious of their life during the time of sleep; and their dream bodies were the ones primarily involved. But the rest of the rebellious part of the cosmos, as well as the less life-enhancing portions of humanity, perished.

This is not visible to us for again, in order to avoid fear, there are many empty, soulless bodies at the time of this writing who are going through the motions of life. However, they cannot sustain the life of their bodies for long without a soul; and many deaths will occur.

2. Those Who Overcome on Earth Become the Leaders

*"And he who overcomes and keeps my words until the
end, to him I will give power over the nations."* <u>Rev. 3:5</u>

With the exception of the two-thirds who rebelled against Mother, those remaining earned the right to govern the cosmos, assuming they also have the highest love, praise and gratitude.

3. The Book of Life

> *"And I saw the dead, small and great, standing before the Goddess and books were opened. And another book was opened, which is the Book of Life. And the dead were judged according to their works, by the things which were written in the books.'* Rev. 20:12

During the months of January through August, 2006, the masters in my classes and I have had almost daily assignments pertaining to the preparation of a book. The book is Mother's book of highest wisdom—a standard to measure how life-enhancing a being is. It is the much-prophesied Book of Life. If a life is lived to the minimum standards of this Book, it earns the right to continue life in the new creation.

> *"He who overcomes shall be clothed in white garments and I will not blot out his name from the Book of Life."*
> Rev. 3:5

White garments refer to the light that is starting to be visible to some, shining around those of pure frequency. Each person had an individual book containing their deeds during their lifetimes in the previous cycle.

4. The Absorption of Life Forms back into the Sea of Consciousness Will Cease

> *"The sea gave up the dead who were in it, and Death and Hades delivered up the dead who were in them. And they were judged each one according to his works. Then Death and Hades were cast into the lake of fire. This is the second death. And anyone not found written in the Book of Life was cast into the lake of fire."*
> Rev. 20: 14,15

The second death, which is the annihilation of individuation or identity, has ceased for all life that has earned the right to be in the new creation. They have earned the opportunity for eternal life. For them, the reality of death is removed—all that is left of death is illusion. Many bodies on earth are empty and need to die, so there will definitely be many bodily deaths. The bodies that have souls in them will die only if their belief systems keep death's illusion in place. This applies to the remaining spirits as well. As we rise into higher levels of energy, these dead will once again be among us. They will not have changed to matter, we will have changed to energy.

5. The Goddess Who Brought Pain and Darkness

"Come, I will show you the judgment of the great harlot who sits on many waters, with whom the kings of the earth committed fornication, and the inhabitants of the earth were made drunk with the wine of her fornication."
Rev. 18: 7, 8

"In the measure that she glorified herself and lived luxuriously, in the same measure give her torment and sorrow for she says in her heart, I sit as queen and am no widow, and will not see sorrow. ...she will be utterly burned with fire, for strong is the Eternal Goddess who judges her." Rev. 18: 7,8

Among the deceivers and bringers of pain, there were dozens of note under the primary male god. Among the females there was one who had planned and plotted to become queen of the cosmos as she observed the kings gathering forces to suppress and injure Mother. She worked from two levels of existence, but nothing could save her, and those she seduced into following her, from the ultimate fate of extinction that awaited her.

There was in fact a time last year when a black hole was deliberately created to cause the minds of the beings in the cosmos to bend.[12] They acted as though drunk. That was when she and some of the dark males persuaded many of the beings in the cosmos to give them their power. In <u>Rev. 3:11</u>, Christ warned: *"Hold fast what you have that no one may take your crown."*

This is also why he told the parable of the foolish virgins who gave away the oil for their lamps and then did not have enough when the bridal procession came. Power yields perception; those who had given their power away did not have enough perception to see through the web of illusion when the final testing of the great rebellion came, and they had to take a stand.

6. The Villainous Gods Perish

> *"The beast was captured and with him the false prophet who worked signs in his presence ... These two were cast alive into the lake of burning brimstone."*
> <u>Rev. 18: 20</u>

This is only one of many, many verses indicating the triumph of good over evil as well as the destruction of the ones of darkness.

7. The Density Becomes an Energy Source

> *"Come and gather together for the supper of the great goddess, that you may eat the flesh of kings, the flesh of captains, the flesh of mighty men ..."* <u>Rev. 20:10</u>

The density of the previous cycle is now an energy source for the beings that have earned the right to live in the new creation. We have described this in the section entitled How to Digest Density as an Energy Source. The light-promoters literally are

12. See *Earth In Ascension* series on CDs.

feeding off the negativity of the god kings of the past.

8. Mother Provides an Unlimited Supply of Awareness

"And she said to me, 'It is done! I am the Alpha and Omega, the Beginning and the End. I will give of the fountain of the water of life freely to him who thirsts."
Rev. 21:6

"And he showed me a pure river of water of life, clear as crystal, proceeding from the throne of the Goddess ... and let him who thirsts come." Rev. 22:1, 17

In the new creation, the Holy Mother provides a never-ending stream of awareness that spreads across the cosmos and is freely available to anyone who has love, praise and gratitude. This is the fountain of living waters referred to in many scriptures.

9. All Things Are Renewed

"And the Goddess will wipe away every tear from their eyes; there shall be no more death, nor sorrow, nor crying. There shall be no more pain, for the former things have passed away." Rev. 21:4, 5

In the 'twinkling of an eye' all things were renewed when we entered the new creation. This reflects that which Mother is; and changes all things from mortal to immortal. Even old patterns or imprints from the past have been removed.

Then She who sat on the throne said, "Behold, I make all things new." Rev. 21:4, 5

About a month before all life was re-formed into the cosmos, Christ had said: *"Soon there shall be a great miracle."* At the time, I did not know what he meant. Now I do. It is with gratitude for his vision and words of hope that I acknowledge that they helped get me through a time during which I thought I could not bear the anguish of the darkness and treachery I had to witness and help reveal.

A great miracle has indeed occurred. Pain is no longer a reality, but an illusion. A long eternal day of joy has dawned.

1.19 The First and Second Resurrections

<u>Rev. 20:46</u>

" ...and I saw the souls of them that were beheaded for
the witness of Jesus and for the word of the Goddess[13]
and which had not worshipped the beast ... and they
lived and reigned with Christ a thousand years.
But the rest of the dead lived not again until the thou-
sand years were finished. This is the first resurrection.
Blessed and holy is he that hath part in the first resur-
rection: on such the second death hath no power but
they shall be priests of the Goddess and of Christ and
shall reign with him ..."

The last cycle of illusion, Prunasvaheresvi, closed at the end of July 2006; and the new creation was birthed in mid-August 2006. However, nine-tenths of Creation still had not earned the right to enter into the new creation. This was the result of a huge rebellion staged by the major gods of the heavens, misleading most in shifting their allegiance away from the Mother of all Creation.

It appeared as we entered the new creation that it had come at

---

13. The word 'God' has been changed to the way it was originally written.

a terrible cost of life; a failure of most to utilize the gift of free-dom of choice in exercising their responsibilities in the last cycle. That cycle had been part of a nine-cycle experiment in which Mother externalized many of her attributes, while keep-ing those within her dormant.

The root of light, for instance, she kept as a dormant function within her and externalized it by giving the task of holding the root of light to the major god. When he became corrupted, it corrupted light everywhere. This was the result of his freedom of choice in the last cycle.

Then in the final week of September 2006, the many bodies that had been walking on earth in a soulless state were once again inhabited by re-formed souls of pristine beauty. The sec-ond resurrection had taken place. All over the cosmos beings re-formed at a much higher level, completely forgetful of dark roles they may have assumed on the grand stage of the previous drama.

Revelations speaks of a thousand years of peace passing between the first and second resurrections. To understand this, one just has to watch children at play on a merry-go-round. The child perched at the middle is hardly moving at all, while the one on the edge is screaming with dizzy delight at the high speed he is traveling.

The earth is the cosmic pivot point. Thousands of years seem like weeks to us in the middle of the merry-go-round. Exactly a thousand years have passed between the 17th of August 2006 and the first week of October 2006. We would have no way of knowing this, of course. Temporarily, the illusion of time and our rotation around the sun continues to be maintained.

Furthermore, Revelations says that the purified ones shall reign with Christ during that time. During August through September 2006 the immortal masters in my classes have had many assignments from the Mother that have fulfilled exactly this prophecy. They have, among many other things, established the cosmic matrices, activated the movement of the cosmic rays of light, helped create Mother's palace, written the new quality of life on earth into the Book of Life and much more.

The fulfillment of humankind's destiny is complete. No longer begging for alms at the gate, they shall take their places on thrones in the presence of the Infinite Goddess in the very near future.

SECTION TWO

The Ring of Healing

2.1 Introduction

Belvaspata, healing of the heart, is a sacred modality that heals with light and frequency. This healing method is a gift from the creator Goddess to the cosmic races to accommodate the changing laws of physics that took place as all life ascended into a new creation in August 2006. The use of Belvaspata heals the environment as the sacred sigils connect the practitioner to the planetary grids. *(Fig. 28, The Sigil for Belvaspata)*

2.2 Belvaspata, the Healing Modality

Belvaspata, the healing modality for the new frequencies within the cosmos, takes into consideration changes that occurred in August 2006, altering the laws governing all existence. The changed frequencies raised us out of a cycle of existence in which polarity was the primary causation for cosmic movement. We entered instead a more elevated cycle of existence in which resonance becomes the basic moving force.

The most basic assumptions on which healers of all modalities have based their methods changed overnight. In the past, **opposite** energies attracted and healing energy gravitated

The Sigil for Bel-vas-pata

Bel-vas-pata
Healing of the Heart

The Over-all Angel for Bel-vas-pata

Kelech-nutva-veleshvispata
Angel sigil:

(Figure 28)

towards diseased energies. Now, they reject each other. Instead, healers can now utilize light and frequency to dispel disease, since under the changed cosmic laws, their opposite aspects attract.

Belvaspata, in the angelic languages of the higher realms now accessible to us, means 'healing of the heart'. Whereas the primary purpose of previous cycles of existence was to seek perception (which is mind-oriented), the one we've entered has a different purpose. This creation challenges us to fulfill one primary purpose: **To create through the heart.**

The body of knowledge, which is Belvaspata, is a gift from the angels that we may fulfill the new purpose of life. It is here to help us create health, joy and happiness through the heart.

2.3 Integrating the Twelve Frequencies

In preparation for Belvaspata's first level initiation, the initiate must integrate the twelve frequencies (emotions) that comprise the twelve frequency bands of the cosmos. At least one whole day should be put aside for this. *(Fig. 29, The Twelve Bands of Emotion) of the Cosmos)*

The Emotions

Each pair of emotions represents a ring and its masculine and feminine aspects. They pulse against each other to enhance the qualities of both. In other words, the stronger one feels a specific emotion, the deeper one can go into its opposite aspect.

Furthermore, the more strongly an emotion is felt, the more its opposite must be experienced or an overbalance results. For instance, if one does not alternate achievement with fun, it can

The Twelve Bands of Emotion of the Cosmos

In the previous cycle light formed the matrix of the cosmos, while emotion and awareness moved. In the new cycle rings of emotion form the matrix. Omnipresent awareness permeates everything.

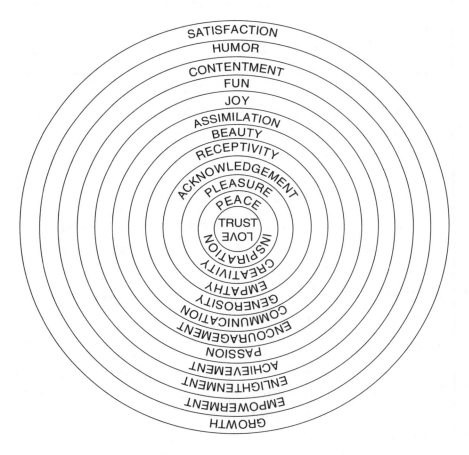

The bands are represented by 12 Goddesses. Each band represents two opposite poles of emotion. The poles pulse each other.

(Figure 29)

become blind ambition, losing sight of the quality of the journey.

It is essential that the steps be performed in the same order as the frequencies are found in their spheres within the cosmos, starting from the core emotions of love and trust, and working your way out to growth and satisfaction.

To internalize an emotion, we approach it from the largest perspective:

- While in a meditative state, visualize your heart center opening wider and wider until you can imagine seeing the whole earth in it.
- Imagine and visualize the heart center opening at a rate beyond the speed of light until the solar system, the galaxy and then many galaxies are visible through the heart.
- Continue opening while in deep meditation until the whole cosmos is within you and you have reached the membrane that contains it all.
- The large central sun will now be within you and you will see its arms of light spiraling outwards, consisting of trillions upon trillions of galaxies like specks of light.
- Remind yourself that you are a consciousness superimposed over all that is and all that you see.
- From this large perspective, feel the frequency of the emotion ripple through you as you envision all that evokes it.
- Sustain it until it is strong, potent and all you can feel.
- When you've become the emotion, understand and observe how it pulses with its opposite aspect.
- When you can feel them both, move on to the next emotion while keeping the expanded awareness.
- Each pair of emotions should be explored and experienced for about half an hour.

The Twelve Pairs of Emotions

Positive Aspect	*Negative Aspect*

1. Love
The desire to include
(replaces fear)

Trust
The desire to surrender

2. Inspiration
The desire to be inspired
and to inspire (replaces anger)

Peace
The desire to be at ease
(replaces protectiveness)

3. Creativity
The desire to create

Pleasure
The desire to be delighted

4. Empathy
The desire to connect

Acknowledgement
The desire to see the perfection

5. Generosity
The desire to give

Receptivity
The desire to receive

6. Encouragement
The desire to encourage
or to be encouraged

Beauty
The desire to be uplifted

7. Communication
The desire to express

Assimilation
The desire to integrate

8. Passion
The desire to know

Joy
The desire to live

9. Achievement
The desire to excel

Fun
The desire to revel

10. Enlightenment
The desire to enhance or
be enhanced (replaces pain)

Contentment
The desire to retain

11. Empowerment	**Humor**
The desire to be of service	The desire to be amused

12. Growth	**Satisfaction**
The desire to expand	The desire to be fulfilled

1. Trust and Love

Trust and Love are the core emotions for the new creation of existence and replace fear.

As old programming of fear breaks down in every being, the new reality of trust must reveal itself. It is, after all, what's real; what is. All else is just an illusion.

Trusting that our lives are guided in every way by our largest identity that spans all existence, we can release our attempts to control life. But what guides our highest self? The One Life that sustains us all; infinite, timeless and vast.

In your expanded state, feel the essence of the One Infinite Being, its serenity, compassion and ageless wisdom. Feel your expanded being as part of this Infinite's vastness and all-encompassing love. This is what runs all life. Allow yourself to surrender to the guidance and love of the Infinite.

The more we surrender to the One, to ourselves, the deeper our love for all beings grows. We can include them in our love because we see so clearly that the roles we play in our experiences are but small ones on a small stage. When we look further, each being is a unique perspective superimposed over all that is—just as vast as we are and just as deserving of life as a part of the Infinite's Being.

Allow love, trust and total surrender to flood your being until they have become part of all you are.

2. Peace and Inspiration

Peace and Inspiration form the second ring, the desire to be at home, to feel totally at ease. These rings build on each other; we cannot feel peace when trust is not present, telling us that life is safe. Peace knows that the cosmos is a safe home; that we can relax in the knowledge that we are in the secure hands of our highest self.

The striving that was part of linear progression in the previous cycle left us feeling we always had to become what we were not. The new creation offers us an unprecedented gift that makes striving unnecessary. All is available right now in terms of awareness. All we have to do is open the door in each moment using the ascension attitudes. These attitudes come when we cease to strive and are fully at ease within the moment.

This deep peace creates our happiness and acceptance of our body as the center of our cosmic home. This is not something lightworkers have generally felt. Many have been unaccustomed to dense bodies, having been seeded into humanity as a gift of light during the earth's pivotal role during the cosmic ascension.

They've wanted to leave their bodies, at times even living partially out of body. Where is there to go if we are everywhere at once? We are neither the body nor its experiences. Secure in this knowledge, we can be at peace and enjoy the play.

This feeling of being at peace within ourselves and at home in the cosmos did not come easily in the previous cycle for another very prominent reason. Since opposites attracted, we were surrounded by opposite energy. The greater our light, the greater the darkness that lurked behind the faces we drew into our environment.

Now that the same energies attract each other, we will be attracting others who live the same high standards of impeccability. We will finally not only feel at home within ourselves but also with others. We must be able to allow those with opposite energies to depart with grace however, for in keeping with the new laws of the cosmos, their departure is inevitable. It's also inevitable that others with like energies must gravitate towards us.

It is in the deep peace of our being we access the perfection of all life. It is here that inspiration is born. We are now immortal in our individuated beings and physical immortality is available also through constant states of the ascension attitudes. We have now every reason to be inspired; to build a life of beauty and a legacy that inspires others.

3. Creativity and Pleasure

The link between Creativity and Pleasure is apparent, as the more pleasure fills our life, the more the muse stirs us into creativity. The more creative we become, the more our pleasure increases.

This pair of emotions, together with that of trust and peace, form the core of the new creation. That such pleasant and worthy emotions have replaced anger, pain, fear and protectiveness is a cause for gratitude and great praise. They form the hub, or core of the rings of frequency, inspiring creativity through love —the primary purpose for life.

To be constantly delighted simply takes full awareness of the moment. When we truly experience the wonder of the senses, the beauty of Creation all around us and the heroism that lies in everyday life, delight will flood our being. Only those unaware or steeped in thought can deprive themselves of the pleasure life so freely offers the one who lives in the moment.

4. Acknowledgement and Empathy

See the ever-unfolding perfection underlying appearances. It isn't enough to acknowledge that the perfection is there, then feel victimized by someone a while later. Do we truly realize that we have co-created whatever is in our life?

If we don't like what we have created, it is now easier for us to make changes since the very purpose of this new paradigm is creating through love. If we focus on that which we love, new creation will flow. If we focus on that which we don't like, the change won't come. In this new creation, therefore, we have come into our spiritual maturity; we have become co-creators with the Infinite. The perfection is not just there for us to **find;** it's ours to create.

How do we create perfection? By finding it in others, in the moment, in the situation. We create that which we love in another. Lightworkers no longer need to be surrounded by those of an opposite energy. It should therefore be easy to see perfection in those we draw into our lives.

When we focus on perfection, our ability to find it increases. Our life will be increasingly filled by a light-family. In the safety of being among others like us, we empathically connect. The opposite aspect of acknowledgement is the desire to connect— empathy.

Encounters with those of lower light also allow a heart connection because we connect with the perfection of their higher selves, not their lowest. In seeing this, we help them to achieve that perfection.

Now it is safe for us to connect empathically with others. We're no longer the martyrs. We no longer have to be injured so others may learn. Because our hearts are open, we've become cosmic creators. This is a role so precious and significant that we cannot allow the last remaining illusion in another to close off this priceless connection we have with all life.

5. Receptivity and Generosity

When a large cycle closes, as has just occurred, not only do opposite aspects reverse but, as a consequence, they also flow. In the previous cycle, lightworkers were surrounded by those who wanted their light. The takers weren't consciously aware of what they were seeking, so they took anything they could get. Lightworkers, therefore, have been giving for ages while others have been taking.

Now the flow has reversed and the debt has to be paid. There is a law of compensation decreeing that imbalance in any part of existence must have an equal and opposite movement to correct it. This is about to happen as lightworkers are repaid for all their giving.

There is just one requirement, however, and that is receptivity. After only giving for so long, lightworkers must break the mindset that can stand in the way of opening to receive. They must, in fact, look forward to it, expect it and envision it.

There has been an agenda associated with others giving to us that has sometimes made us reluctant to receive. But if it is the cosmos settling a score, we are really getting what belongs to us by rights. What does it then matter through what means it chooses to repay us? Let us be filled with receptivity.

When we give, we must not think that such generosity depletes us. Rather let us see how generosity and receptivity form one long continuous flow. Though the wind blowing through the house enters at the window, it leaves through the door.

Express both receptivity and generosity joyously.

6. Beauty and Encouragement

It can be said that beauty is just a glimpse into the perfection of the indwelling life behind form. It sees that which has enduring value, like a doorway into eternity. Every time we recognize beauty, we are encouraged (encouragement being its opposite aspect).

Beauty encourages us to create our life as a living work of art. If we see ourselves surrounded by beauty, we are hallowed by it. Moments become meaningful. A hard journey through life becomes not only tolerable, but we feel encouraged enough to believe we can flourish rather than survive.

There are obvious visions of beauty; the sunset over the sea, a child's sleeping face, a new kitten. But the true disciple of beauty doesn't stop there. Encouraged by what has become a treasure hunt for gems of beauty, he seeks to find them in the most unlikely places.

Artists of old saw beauty in the mundane, in another man's trash. They painted the crumbs of a left-over meal, the spill of a wineglass. For where others saw only dirty dishes, the artist saw light as it played on crystal and wine and reflected off a wayward spoon.

They did not paint objects, but a dance of light, playfully leading the eye of the observer across the canvas of a captured moment. A famous English watercolorist said at the end of his life that he had never seen anything ugly. These are the words of a true disciple.

7. Assimilation and Communication.

Too little true assimilation of information (which is accessed light) takes place in the world for several reasons.

- True listening to another's words can only take place in the absence of internal dialog. The listener has to stay in the silence of the mind and enter into the other's viewpoint by feeling the communication with the heart.
- The past cycle was left-brain dominated, but the non-verbal communications from the right brain accessed 9 times more than did the left brain. The subtle information from the cosmos around us got crowded out by thought.
- Finding silence is getting more and more difficult. Airplanes roar, car horns blare, appliances hum and then, as though that were not enough, TVs are on whether someone is watching or not. Cell phones make sure that no one has silent time around them. But it is in silence that we get to know ourselves through listening to our thoughts and desires.
- Conversation and inter-generational communication has dwindled in most cultures where TV has become the substitute for knowing one another.
- We spend too little time in appreciation of nature's wonders, and much of that experience has become action-oriented. All of the natural world and its creatures speak to us through their individual frequencies. We can assimilate their special life

song by sitting in silence and feeling it within our cells.

The assimilation of other's communications enriches us. Their diversity can carve new facets in our own life, new perspectives that leave us enhanced. When we feel truly heard, the desire to communicate (its opposite aspect) becomes more active as well.

8. Passion and Joy

When the social conditioning of our lives has left the clear impression that it is unsafe to fully participate in the game of life, we may hang back in the safety of the known, afraid to make ourselves a target by being noticed. We may fear that passion could cause our light to shine so brightly that others might try and tear us down so that their own lack of luster isn't as obvious.

If we deny our desire to express passionately long enough, we end up being strangers to passion; not knowing how to find it nor recognize it even if we do. The lateral hypothalamus tells us when we have eaten enough. The ventromedial hypothalamus tells us when we are hungry. In the same way, if we deny the promptings from these portions of the brain, we will end up either obese or anorexic. When that happens we have to gently coach ourselves into recalling how their promptings feel.

When passion beckons, we feel warm and excited; our faces flush and our imagination stirs with questions of "What if?" and "What lies beyond the next horizon?" It inspires us into action and makes us believe we can take risks and build.

We find our passion by following the yearnings our moments of joy evoke within our hearts. It is the lost song the singer feels hiding within the shadows of his mind; the lost rhythm the dancer forever seeks; the mysteries of the cosmos that wait for the scientist or the metaphysician to unlock. It is the desire, inspired by the innocence in our child's eyes, to build a life of wonder and beauty for our family.

If passion has become a stranger to us, we may need to become re-acquainted with it one facet at a time. When it is expressed, passion consists of taking risks. It is the precursor to accomplishment and the building of something new. It adds new experiences, further boundaries, and new depth to our lives.

To train ourselves to hear the voice of passion again, we find the yearning of our heart and follow where it leads. We make a concerted effort to break free from the prison bars of ruts and expectations, socially conditioned limitations and self-imposed belief systems that keep us in mediocrity. We take a few minutes a day to dare to dream of what would make our hearts sing. We awake each morning and determine to live the day before us as though it were our last. We look at our lives as though for the first time, with a fresh perspective that can detect the joyless, self-sacrificing areas. With courage and great consideration for the consequences of our actions on others, we implement our first steps to bring the glow of passion back to these areas.

A decision may take a minute to make, but for it to be as life-altering as we would want it to be, it must be supported by a firm foundation. This requires planning and a certain amount of analysis. What is the goal? What resources will be needed? Is there a discrepancy between what we need and what we have? How can we fill it? Many businesses fail, taking many dreams with them, because not enough thought was given to what was needed to support them in terms of time and money. Once a goal is identified, break it into projects and tasks.

Many envy the achievements of others, but are not prepared to put in the work. Sometimes it takes burning the candle on both ends to fulfill a dream. It is our passion that keeps our enthusiasm lit and gives us our second wind to fly higher than we ever thought possible.

As passion explores the multitude of possibilities through which we can express, so joy is concentrated on the simplicity of the moment. Joy is a mindset, a certain focus that sees the perfection of the here and now, casting a golden glow over the experiences of yesterday. It turns the mundane into poetry and captures the moment in a still life image.

Milton said: *"The mind in its own place and of itself can turn hell into heaven and heaven into hell"*. The great English master painter, Turner, at the end of his life said that in his entire life he'd never seen anything ugly. Franz Lizt was urged to write his memoirs, but he said: *"It's enough to have lived such a life"*. He found such joy in his experiences, he didn't have to externalize them to appreciate them.

Joy can be recognized by the deep feeling of satisfaction it brings; by the feeling that one has come home to oneself. It taps into the quiet place within that nurtures the soul and replenishes the mind. When we are under its spell, joy makes us feel light and young again, connected to the earth and freed from our cares.

Just as building with passion requires careful and disciplined time allocations, living with joy requires us to focus on the details in front of us at the moment. Even if we cannot find even a moment today to do the things we enjoy, we can find the time to enjoy the things we are doing. In cutting up vegetables to make a stew, we can see the colors of the carrots, explore the different textures of each vegetable, smell the fresh fragrance as we cut through their skins.

Even repetitive work can become a mantra, or a production line a prayer as we send blessings and angelic assistance to the homes where the products will end up. Walking in the crowded street, we can feel the sadness of others but can turn it into joy by envisioning blessings pouring into their lives. The loss in the lives of others can be used to inspire praise and gratitude for the blessings in our own.

In our choice of the joy to fill our leisure time, we look for that which will inspire us into accomplishment. As the joy flows inward on the surface, the passion it inspires folds outward beneath the surface. The greater our joy, the greater the actions it will inspire.

9. Fun and Achievement

We've possibly all heard the saying that someone we know 'works hard and plays hard'. That's because the two go hand in hand. Fun without achievement is a shallow, unfulfilling life. Achievement without the fun that brings quality to the journey leads to an equally unsatisfying life. Blind ambition can result from such an imbalance and one becomes blinded as to which achievements would be truly life-enhancing.

Fun helps energy flow and prevents us from taking ourselves too seriously. It relieves the tensions we experience during our battles of achievement.

10. Contentment and Enlightenment

Contentment knows that it is living perfect moments; the fire is crackling in the fireplace, a little child with sleep-weighted eyelids is wrapped in a quilt on your lap, while the rain of a winter night beats outside on the windowpanes.

It is during those moments that we wish everyone on earth could share the feeling—complete contentment. We wish we could enhance the life of a runaway teenager somewhere in a lonely bus station. We want to have the hungry family in the ghetto fed and feeling the inner fulfillment contentment brings.

Such contentment can come as a strong under-current of life, rather than as a few fleeting moments. Contentment as a constant companion is the result of deep, meaningful living; of insights gained and inner storms weathered. The desire to enhance and enlighten the life of another is the sincere wish that insight will change despair into contentment for another as well.

11. Empowerment and Humor

Empowerment is the desire to serve. At first, this definition might not make sense. The connection between service and empowerment might seem a bit obscure. The reason is that man has really not understood the proper meaning of service.

Service has often meant assuaging our conscience by giving a handout, not really addressing the deficiency that caused the condition in the first place. True service instead is empowering the individual to find his own way out of the dire straits of his life. This way he has something to show for his hardship; new-found strength or abilities.

The desire to be of service will be never-ending if it is based

on need. As Christ said, "The hungry will always be among us."
It could eventually pull us into the despair of need as well. The
balancing factor is humor.

Humor laughs at life, laughs at self and, instead of blaming,
laughs at the folly of others. It cannot take anything too seriously because it knows without a shadow of doubt that we're just
engaged in a play. It helps by empowering the beggar, not
because he seems needy, but just because it is his role. The play
must go on because it has value.

12. Growth and Satisfaction

Understanding the essence of growth is new. This is because
the way growth now takes place is new. It used to be the result
of delving (painfully, at times) into the unknown, grappling
with its illusion and eventually turning it into the known
through experience. When delving into the unknown, fear
resulted, often bringing about protectiveness. When the illusion
refused to yield its insights, anger tried to break it up.

The emotions associated with growth weren't always pleasant
and even the word 'growth' often had an unpleasant connotation.
Growth is now an expansion that is the result of satisfaction.

When we are with those who are energetically incompatible,
we experience a shrinking feeling. The new creation brings kin-
dred spirits in the form of family and friends. In the deep satisfaction of their company, we can feel our souls expand.

Growth used to come through opposition. Now it comes
through support. How will we know when we've found it? The
deep satisfaction of our hearts will tell us we've just lived our
highest truth.

2.4 Symbols vs. Sigils

To familiarize ourselves with the power of the goddess symbols, we must first understand what symbols entail. We will also need to know the meanings of sigils in order to properly understand and utilize them as they are given later in this book.

A symbol represents something, whereas a sigil describes something. When someone sees a BMW or a Mercedes symbol, it represents upper middle-class vehicles of quality and distinction. On the other hand, the symbol for a Rolls Royce or Bentley represents elite vehicles that speak of a privileged lifestyle of dignity and wealth.

So much is deduced just from one symbol. A Rolls Royce evokes images of walled estates, chauffeurs, enough and accustomed money as opposed to the symbol of a Ferrari which speaks of more flamboyant taste.

Whereas symbols are common in our everyday world, the use of sigils is virtually forgotten. Even in mystery schools, their hidden knowledge eludes most mystics. But throughout the cosmos all beings of expanded awareness utilize sigils and only a few left-brain oriented races use symbols and those primarily in alphabets. The reason is this:

If we use the world 'LOVE', we have combined four symbols (letters representing certain sounds) to make one symbol (the word that represents a feeling). But love is one of the building blocks of the cosmos, like space or energy[14]. It can also represent many different nuances within the emotion of love (the desire to include) and many other dis-functionalities and degrees of need we mistakenly call 'love'. *(Figs. 30, 31, 32, Sigils of Love)*

14. Discussed in *Journey to the Heart of God*, p. 56, The True Nature of the Seven Directions

Sigils of Love*

These sigils are used in pairs to stimulate healthy frequency.

+

Inspiration / Angel name
Kriavat-bishpi

*use in areas of
red rash, redness,
or inflamation*

−

Peace / Angel name
Pele-nanvabruk

+

Enlightenment / Angel name
Grunachberesvikvit

use for pain

−

Contentment / Angel name
Kletsatvarabuch

+

Love / Angel name
Perech-pri-parva

*use for obesity
and flab*

−

Trust / Angel name
Truessabru-varabi

+

Passion / Angel name
Gelkrig-sutvra-bararech

*use for poor
circulation*

−

Joy / Angel name
Travi-usbava

---

* *Initiates for Level II need to prepare for a day by internalizing these emotions.*

(Figure 30)

Continued: Sigils of Love

+

Generosity / Angel name
Teshvinechspi-urarat

*use in reduce
blood pressure*

−

Receptivity / Angel name
Nenhursh-brechbravit

+

Empathy / Angel name
Flelvi-respi-uhuru-vak

injuries

−

Acknowledgement / Angel name
Tre-uch-vara-vaar

+

Communication / Angel name
Araragatveshpi

lungs

−

Assimilation / Angel name
Nun-heresch-vispi

+

Achievement / Angel name
Gele-vish-tra-va

*throat,
thyroid*

−

Fun / Angel name
Pru-eshbi-klechvaha

(Figure 31)

+

Empowerment / Angel name
Bu-esbi-klechnatra

*digestive tract,
elimination,
kidneys, adrenals*

−

Humor / Angel name
veluchvespri-rekva

+

Encouragement / Angel name
Kletsut-vesba

*pancreas' liver'
gallbladder*

−

Beauty / Angel name
Nunberesh-nuk

+

Creativity / Angel name
Veles-vruchba

*Genitals,
reproductive
organs*

−

Pleasure / Angel name
Prubechba-natruva

+

Growth / Angel name
Trubi-kluvespraha

*bones, fractures,
muscles, joints*

−

Satisfaction / Angel name
Nechtruavar

(Figure 32)

As we can see, the symbol or word can be very misleading since what it represents to one may not be what it represents to another. The sigil for love describes the quality or frequency of what is meant. It maps out the exact frequency of the emotion.

The sigil for someone's name would do the same. As the person or being rises in frequency, the sigil will change to reflect that. In the case of angels, even their names change. That is why the angel names or the goddess names have changed as the cosmos and earth have ascended to a much higher frequency[15]. In these higher realms the languages are different and reflect the higher frequencies.

When a person has accomplished a major task within the cosmos pertaining to the agreement they made with the Infinite, they also receive a 'meaning' with its accompanying sigil. When a being is called to do a task meant for the highest good, that being will come if you have its name and meaning. The being absolutely **must** come if, in addition, you have the sigil for the name and meaning.

Having someone's sigil is like having that person's phone number. Sigils not only describe what they represent, but are a means to communicate with what they represent.

2.5 The Significance of the Sigils

If all other healing modalities are having their healing energy, and their symbols meant to produce healing energy repulsed, they are in fact producing the opposite of what is intended.

Because disease is distorted energy that repulses the natural healing energies (the trillions of little fragments of awareness

15. See higher goddess names in *Secrets of the Hidden Realms*

that have been available to restore perfection), these methods would produce disease.

On August 17, 2006, in order to prevent well-intentioned healers from doing harm, the masters took away the power behind healing modalities based on energy work. The power behind the previously used symbols was also removed. It is for this reason that the gift of Belvaspata was given to humanity.

2.6 The Significance of the Master Sigil

The master sigil is to be used only for initiations of master practitioners because of the following purpose held within its power:

The sigils of Belvaspata have a hidden power behind the obvious. Every time they're used, they dispel the illusion of disease and the illusion of distortions found everywhere in light and frequency. In other words, when these sigils are used there is less disease everywhere on earth. The master sigil extends this influence to the whole cosmos. (*Figs. 33–38, Initiation Sigils for Belvaspata*)

After having practiced the sigils regularly and above all, internalized the true emotions and rays of light, a Level II practitioner becomes connected through this sigil to the grid of existence that spans the cosmos. Practicing Belvaspata, therefore, becomes a cosmic service, bringing healing to life everywhere.

Where great service is rendered, great rewards are given. The rewards in this instance are that the sigils previously placed in the centers of the practitioner's body during Level I and Level II initiations, now work 100 times more effectively as the master uses them. A second magnificent reward is higher conscious-

Initiation Sigils Level I Bel-vas-pata Healing Modality
(Healing of the Heart)

All 3 sigils are used to start every healing.

1.

Kel-a-visva-uravech
Release of patterns that no longer serve (transformation)

angel sigil:

To be done 3 times over lower abdomen.
Call in the angel: Krunechva-atruha

2.

Trech-su-ba-reshvi
Transmuting matter to light

angel sigil:

To be done 3 times over solar plexus
Call in angel: Mirakluvael

3.

Pata-uru-hut-vi
Transfiguring illusion to light

angel sigil:

To be done 3 times over sternum
Call in angel: Kelevi-traunar

(Figure 33)

106

Initiation Sigils Level II

(When healing use in conjunction with Level I's
sigils to start the session)

1.

To be done 3 times over lower abdomen.
Call in the angel: Krunechva-atruha

Kel-a-visva-uravech
Release of patterns that no
longer serve (transformation)

angel sigil:

2.

To be done 3 times over solar plexus
Call in angel: Mirakluvael

Trech-su-ba-reshvi
Transmuting matter to light

angel sigil:

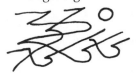

3.

Pata-uru-hut-vi
Transfiguring illusion to light

angel sigil:

To be done 3 times over sternum
Call in angel: Kelevi-traunar

(Figure 34)

4.

Kers-baur-veshpi
Sanctification

angel sigil:

To be done 3 times over crown
angel name: Trechbar-uru-heresvi

5.

Klet-sut-manarech
Attracting light into the
voice over throat

angel sigil:

To be done 3 times over throat
angel name: Vilivesbi-keres-na

6.

Vis-beles-pah-rech-vi
Attracting healing frequencies
into the hands

angel sigil:

To be done 3 times in each hand
angel name: Kru-echna-vilshpreva

(Figure 35)

7.

Nen-hersh-bi-klet-rasut
DNA Activation

angel sigil:

*To be done 3 times over root chakra
angel name:* Ku-ulu-vet

8.

Vele-echs-bi-kluatret
Creating movement in light

angel sigil:

*To be done 3 times over alpha chakra
one hand length below base of the spine
angel name:* Belech-his-pavatra

Also call in the angel Kelipretvaha *for placing this sigil into the earth.*

9.

Nun-mer-stararot-belsh-spi
Bringing in the new template
of frequency

angel sigil:

*Do 3 times over bottom of each foot
angel name:* Kretna-ulu-vesbi

(Figure 36)

Initiation Mastery Level III

This sigil is not to be used on patients
It is for practitioners only

Bel-veres-nuk-vi
All becomes One

Do 3 times over each of the following: (in order given)

1. bottom of each foot

2. alpha chakra

3. root chakra

4. lower abdomen

5. navel

6. solar plexus

7. heart

8. sternum

9. throat

10. forehead

11. crown

12. both hands

13. 10″ above crown

angel name: Ur-hetvi

angel sigil:

(Figure 37)

110

Closing Sigils to End a Session

Praise

Love

Gratitude

(Figure 38)

ness for the practitioner and greater silence of the mind, which is mastery.

Disease as an Illusion

Initiates into Belvaspata must very clearly understand why disease and the false emotions of anger, fear, pain and protectiveness are, at this point, an illusion. The reminder that healing is but the removal of illusion needs to be done with every use of the sigils. To treat disease as a real adversary is to strengthen illusion.

In 2005 the 'real' part, the indwelling life of disease, was removed. To demonstrate this, if I put my pen on the table and one of the masters of the unseen realms removes the etheric or 'real' pen, it would no longer be real.

I can still pick up the pen and write with it, but some days I may not see it and then one day it will have disappeared altogether. It will, in fact, disappear even quicker if my thinking it's on the table were to stop.

2.7 Guidelines for Belvaspata Healing Modality

- Understand and be able to explain to an initiate the difference between a symbol and a sigil.
- You don't have to sign the angel sigils in the air—just look at them as you call their name.
- The sigils done over the body parts and for initiation—you don't have to memorize them, but can copy them either from a paper held in the left hand or you can place a paper over the area and trace the sigil with your finger.
- The sigils are drawn from left to right. Start at the upper left hand corner. After that the order isn't crucial.

- The language used is a very high cosmic language used by the angels and throughout the god realms.
- There should be at least a three-month time lapse between Level I and Level II initiations. There should be a six-month lapse between Level II and Mastery, with use of the sigils at least twice a week.
- It has to be clearly understood that this modality does not work with energy and matter but rather with light and frequency. The modality has been brought forth to replace previous methods as a result of the change in cosmic laws of attraction that occurred August 11, 2006 in connection with the cosmic ascension.
  - With energy and matter, opposites now repel. Healing energy will therefore be rejected, whereas it was previously received.
  - With light and frequency, opposites now attract. Light will therefore be drawn to illusion, and frequency will be received in areas of distortion.
- Certification may be provided for initiated practitioners. You may charge the same as you do for Reiki. The only exchange I ask for from you and from those whom you train, is an acknowledgement that the information originated from me. If it would enhance the value of the modality in advertising, you may freely reprint any of the endorsements (or portions thereof) from the back of my books.
- Provide training to initiates on how to change the old ways of 'sending energy' into the body, to using the 12 new pairs of emotional frequencies and expanded perception. They need to prepare for initiations by internalizing the new emotions and light.

2.8 Embodying The Sixteen Rays of Light

The root of Light is the Infinite; the Goddess Mother of all Creation. She is like the white light that splits into colors, but in the new creation into which we have entered, there aren't just seven colors in the rainbow, there are sixteen. Whether our minds can initially grasp and interpret that we are seeing colors never before seen, we are nevertheless in a new color spectrum. *(Fig. 39, Sixteen Rays of Light Moving in the Cosmos)*

On August 25, 2006 an unprecedented event happened on earth: sixteen gods of Amenti were called to represent and embody these sixteen rays. What is unique about this event is that for the first time, these gods were chosen from those who are embodied. Sixteen men and women who have entered the god-kingdom[16] on earth, were called to be the new gods and goddesses of Amenti.

The previous seven Lords of Amenti, who have represented the seven rays of light for trillions of years,[17] had completed their cycle of service. It was time for an embodiment that would represent the new nature of light. Previously, light reflected the static grid-work of the cosmos; now it reflects cosmic movement.

The Sixteen Rays in a Clockwise Position:

1. The Root

During this cycle of existence Mother, the Source of all light, is keeping the root of light herself. The purity and incorruptible nature of her Being henceforth safeguards the Cosmic Light against distortion. *(Figs. 40, 41, 42, Sigils of Light)*

As we seek to internalize the root of light in our lives, let us

16. See Stages of Man, 3.1.
17. See chapter describing the Seven Lords of Light in *Journey to the Heart of God*.

Sixteen Rays of Light Moving in the Cosmos

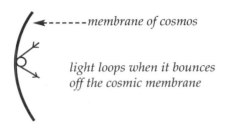

membrane of cosmos

light loops when it bounces off the cosmic membrane

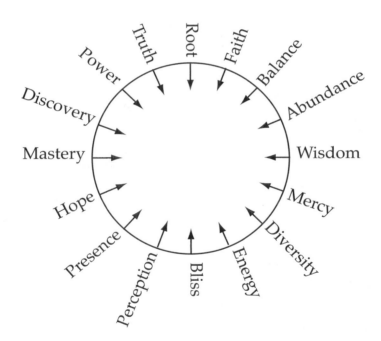

The sixteen rays of light, representing certain attributes, bounce of the border of the cosmos. In the new cosmic cycle, light moves and emotional frequency bands and awareness are static.

(Figure 39)

115

Sigils of Light*

Can be used in a circle. Place sigils in order clockwise.

1.

Root/Lord name
Herhut-brasta

*always use in
conjunction with others*

2.

Faith/Lord name
Belblutvakreshbi

*systemic
illness*

3.

Balance/Lord name
Kluch-nenuvit

*ears, throat,
nose*

4.

Abundance/Lord name
Petrevusbi

*prostate,
rectum*

5.

Wisdom/Lord name
Gelvi-veshbi

*pineal,
hypothalamus*

6.

Mercy/Lord name
Truavar

*spine, occipital
area/base of skull*

7.

Diversity/Lord name
Plu-akbar

*DNA, chromosomes,
memory*

* *Initiates for Level II need to prepare for a day by internalizing these qualities.*

(Figure 40)

8.

Energy / Lord name
Trechvarvulesbi

*blood sugar,
blood purification*

9.

Bliss / Lord name
Besbrakva

*cellular light,
oxygen and ph of cells*

10.

Perception / Lord name
Telenuchvraha

*eyes, pituitary,
3rd eye*

11.

Presence / Lord name
Petrevusbi

legs and feet

12.

Hope / Lord name
Telenuchvraha

*heart,
circulation*

13.

Mastery / Lord name
Brishnavak

*brain, clarity of
thought*

14.

Discovery / Lord name
Vere-bisma

*Tongue, teeth,
tonsils*

(Figure 41)

Continued: Sigils of Light

15.

Power/Lord name
Plu-akbar

skull, scalp, hair

16.

Truth/Lord name
Petluch-vraha

*arms, elbows,
hands/wrists,
shoulders*

Use for Emotional Health

Depression

Angel: Nechvikrechbar

(Figure 42)

be always mindful that we exist in the holiness of her Being and that we can dedicate every action, every breath we take in love, praise and gratitude to the One Being that sustains us and gives us life.

In meditation, let us see ourselves become as vast as the cosmos and as we linger there, let us know we have become one with the Infinite Mother; that in such expanded awareness, we are being cradled in her loving arms. It is here where we will find the source of all light.

2. Faith

This ray is represented by the goddess of Faith. The nature of faith has changed for this creation. Formerly, it was a mindset that re-created itself. In other words, the most prevalent and dominant thoughts ended up creating our environment. Because our thoughts were generally chaotic, we created chaotic conditions on earth.

The new creations don't come through thought, but through the heart. We create through love, praise and gratitude—a way that prevents us from creating more chaos. Faith, as a way to create our reality, has to therefore reflect this change.

The new way to understand faith would be as the conscious creation of reality through an attitude of love. Envision how you would like to live life, and flood the images with love, praise and gratitude that such joyous manifestations can be yours.

3. Balance

The light-ray of balance, presided over by the Goddess of Balance, represents the essence of what the Mayans call "Movement and Measure". Balance is not static, but rather consists of the dynamic movement between expanding boundaries.

In other words, it moves between positive and negative aspects within existence, always pulling them slightly further apart.

As an example, a balanced life pulses between beingness and doingness. The deeper we enter into the peace of our being, the more we can accomplish with our actions (our 'doingness'). In this way, both our passive and pro-active aspects are strengthened and enhanced. In these deepening pulsations, lies the expansion and growth of the being.

4. Abundance

The true meaning of abundance embodied by the Goddess has been colored by the beautiful and uplifting purpose of our new existence, creation through the heart. Before, we hoped that life would deliver abundance. Now we are limited only by how large we can dream and how much love we can pour into our dreams and visions.

While doing this, we continue to broadcast heartfelt gratitude throughout the cosmos for what we want. Increase doesn't occur where there's an absence of gratitude for present gifts. Conversely, whatever we're grateful for increases.

Generosity also increases supply. If we truly understand that we are co-creators of our realities, then our supply has no limit. In giving, we simply open the sluices of manifestation a little wider. If we have love, praise and gratitude, we open it wider still, clustering awareness into manifesting our created realities.

5. Wisdom

This principle is embodied by the God of Wisdom. It has been said that wisdom is applied knowledge. Previously we had to interpret principles that lay hidden within the illusion of the former cycle of existence. Now all illusion has been solved and the new creation lies before us like a pristine uncharted land. What knowledge is there to apply?

The knowledge that needs to be interpreted through our lives is the knowledge of self we see mirrored within those of like energy. In them we see ourselves and learn about what we are. Learning by observing those energies in others, we become more of what we are and find new ways of applying them in our lives.

6. Mercy

The Goddess of Mercy embodies this very beautiful principle. Mercy no longer means tolerating the dysfunctional in our midst. In fact, the opposite is true. Because opposite light and frequency (emotion) now attract, the most merciful way of living is to surround ourselves with authentic, love-filled people who make our hearts sing. As we feel joy, it is automatically drawn to its opposite aspect, the most joyless places in the cosmos.

Mercy therefore resembles a form of 'tough love', a refusal to indulge the clinging to old patterns of illusion as some will want to do. The repelling of those of opposite energies, used to be considered 'uncharitable'. Now not living our highest truth is.

7. Diversity

The greatest period of growth for any group of beings is when there is unity within diversity; in other words interdependency.[18] The slowest growth and ultimately, stagnation, occurs when there is uniformity. We see this in tribal life. The dynamic within the group is one of dependency, keeping its members in an infantile state.

Because the new creation stresses 'sameness', diversity with-

18. See section on Social Stages in *Journey*.

121

in the 'sameness' is absolutely vital. If this were not the case, the possibility of over-polarization into the known (accessed light) would be a very real concern. The inevitable result of such over-polarization is stagnation.

Although we are to study the beautiful qualities of others, we are in fact studying our own. We can only recognize that which we have within—the major reason why light-promoters have been so easily deceived by those of ill-intent. Although what we see is what we are, every other person is like a uniquely colored lens through which his beam of light shines. When this diversity is observed and appreciated, it brings richness to our lives. This ray of light is represented by the Goddess of diversity.

8. Energy

This god was immaculately conceived by the Mother of Creation and is currently in embryonic state. The deep secret behind this fact is that matter and energy have merged. This has already occurred. The gods and goddesses in human form have become 100% energy and are moving into becoming light.

A whole new reality is being born, one in which the Mother Goddess herself will reign on this most pivotal planet, Earth.

9. Bliss

The Goddess of Bliss has immaculately conceived the God of Hope (God of the 12th ray). Bliss is a result of a vast expansive perception that effects the vibration of a body's cells. It is a state of profound praise, love and gratitude generated by an eternal perspective.

The gift of bliss is that old patterns melt away in its presence; constrictions in the flow of energy release. Others experience healings and growth by grace. It is therefore understandable that in a new creation where we are able to access all awareness without effort and by grace through the ascension attitudes, that bliss is present. As one of the rays of light, it offers growth through grace and births hope that anyone can achieve the pinnacle of enlightenment through love, praise and gratitude.

10. Perception

Perception used to come through the gifts of challenge and hardship. Through the friction of life's experiences turning the unknown into the known, perception exacted a high cost.

In the cycle of existence just completed, perception yielded emotion as the primary way of promoting change. Perception birthed the realities of our lives. In this creation, our emotions primarily steer our course, affecting our perception. The more profound our emotions, the more they birth our hopes and dreams into reality.

Imagine our lives as a sphere of existence filled with twelve concentric circular frequency bands (emotion). If the emotions strengthen, the bands expand. Light rays bounce through these bands. If they expand, the light rays have to move through a larger sphere; therefore they have to move faster to complete their pattern. The more intense the emotion, the faster we get our perception.

11. Presence

The Mother of All has a specific 'flavor' to her light; a personality or a color that expresses her Being in this cycle of Creation more than any other. Within this ray of light, the presence of the Infinite Divine Being is accessed and known.

The stillness of Mother's ancient moments, timeless and eternal, the tempestuousness of her cataclysmic change, all can be felt through this ray. The reflections of the facets of her **Being** are reflected in the stupendous variety and exquisite beauty of her creations. We can study the Mother's being by seeing her face in the reflections of the cosmos.

The study and interpretation of the majesty and glory of the Infinite Mother is really the study of self. We are her facets, her reflections. We can only recognize in her what we are in ourselves. This creation is dedicated to studying the known; that which we are. The goddess representing this ray encourages us to study the known by accessing it within the divine presence of the Mother of Creation.

12. Hope

This ray is represented by an infant God on earth. Hope is a state of mind that lives with eyes and heart firmly fixed on the most beneficial outcome. Hope has taken on a entirely new meaning since our reason for being has become creation of that which we love through the heart.

Hope is the vision we hold as we fan the flame of its creation through love, praise and gratitude. This substance is formed of the tiny fragments of awareness that always existed, but have now become abundantly available for us to create with.

As previously described, the attitudes of ascension are really the positive aspects of awareness. The awareness particles comprise the opposite (negative) aspect. Because awareness consists of both love (frequency) and light, where opposites attract, the little rays rush towards the ascension attitudes' source. Here they roll upon themselves according to the mould created by hope.

13. Mastery

The God of Mastery advocates a life lived from complete

authenticity, self-discipline, and inner balance. Mastery is a combination of many attributes that take dedication and focus to achieve. Previously these attributes took years to cultivate, one painstaking step at a time.

With awareness immediately available and with time's collapse into the moment, mastery is now at our fingertips. It takes a mindset that always acts from our highest vision; always remembering that we are a vast being, superimposed over all that is and that wherever we are is the center of our cosmos.

Mastery acts with the utmost impeccability and sensitivity in realizing that every action, every thought impacts the whole. With such an awareness, each act becomes an act of love for the interconnectedness of all life.

14. Discovery

This ray, represented by an immaculately conceived God still in embryo within the Goddess of Mercy, will be parented not only by this Goddess but also by the God of Mastery and the Goddess of Abundance. The great significance of the introduction of this ray of light into Creation is as follows:

The previous cycles of creation were descension cycles, containing a great deal of distorted light. The descension was due to self-centered and separative patriarchal rule. This distorted emotion created fear, anger, pain as well as protectiveness. Thus we were driven further and further down into density.

It did not have to be this way. Mother had given freedom of choice to her creations—an experiment that ended in the destruction of nine tenths of the cosmos[19]. The choices of her creations brought about these painful descension cycles and

19. See The First and Second Resurrections, 1.24.

ultimate rebellion and destruction. The way it was meant to be was through joyful discovery of the unknown, much the same way the ancient mariners set forth to explore the uncharted seas. It was supposed to be a treasure hunt; finding the gems of our own being-ness lying in the dust of the unknown. Through many of the choices made by the higher gods, the adventure of discovery became a nightmare.

The re-installation of this precious ray of light is a wonderful gift as we study the known.

15. Power

This ray of light is held by a baby god immaculately conceived by Mother herself and who is being carried for Mother by the Goddess of Peace.

In the old cycle, lord Ardal held all the other lords' light jointly.

In the new creation, all of the previous rays of light moved into the ray of Power, which then moved to birth the 16th ray, as follows:

- All previous rays moved into the one ray, namely the ray of Power.
- The one ray of Power then moved into the inner emotional sphere of trust/love with the brilliance of all fifteen rays.
- The great power and light caused the emotional sphere to spin counterclockwise.
- The rapid spinning shot out all fifteen previous rays plus an additional one, a pink ray embodying absolute truth.

The first fifteen rays previously mentioned were originally meant to become available as the cosmos ascended. This would have provided the cosmos the ability to move on to a new existence beyond (as we have just done) without having to go through numerous and repetitive cycles of ascension and decension. Due to the distortion chosen by some of the lords of the light rays at the very pinnacle of existence, the additional rays were never given by the Mother of Creation until now.

16. Truth

Embodied by a living Goddess, this newly born ray of truth is a new form of this principle. Truth was previously that which was sought without, through the phantoms of illusion, clustered about and attracted to our light. Truth is no longer found without—after all, we are in a play that has yet to be written. There are no pre-conceived guidelines here. It lies before us, pristine as this new-born ray of truth. This ray is the firstborn child of the cosmos; to be felt in our hearts as the ring of truth.

2.9 How to Heal With Belvaspata

1. Sign the sigil for opening the mind over the forehead one time. Silently call the angel name while looking at the angel sigil (saying the angel name is optional)
2. Do the same as in # 1 for the opening of the heart, signing it once over the heart center.
3. Repeat the steps above for the Receptivity of the Body sigil.

These three steps start every session.

4. Level I sigils must be done over the correct body parts, as described above,. Level II sigils can be done as needed at practitioner's discretion and wherever needed.
5. The sigils of Light and the sigils of Love are used over the afflicted body part as needed.
6. Comb the body's light bodies when the patient is receptive and relaxed, by running the hands from head to toes 6" above

the body. Feel where light is needed.

7. Place your hands either on the client's abdomen or head—or above if laws[20] in your area do not permit touching.

8. Envision yourself expanding and expanding until you are as vast as the cosmos. Hold that expanded awareness for at least 20 minutes.

9. See your client expanding as well until you are both a consciousness blended as one with all that is. Hold that vision.

10. See the client's body within the vastness (just give it or the afflicted area slight intention). Don't focus on it—keep the expansion.

11. Now bring the predetermined pair of emotions (depending on what you felt was needed) into your awareness. Feel it ripple through all the cosmos, generated by you. Stay expanded –don't do the sigils yet.

12. Only when you pull your awareness back before you end the session do you draw the sigils of love and light, as you feel necessary, above the body.

13. Always end a session by signing the sigils for love, praise and gratitude above the client. This materializes the healing intentions and pulls awareness in.

14. Other than when signing sigils and calling in angels at the beginning and end of the session, the state of expansion is maintained throughout. This is the opposite of obsolete methods that focused energy.

Note: Gentle background meditational music helps. No neon or harsh lights. Minimize background noise, it pulls you and the client out of the moment.

---

20. Getting a valid minister's license (research the internet) may make it permissible to touch.

2.10 Self-Initiation into Belvaspata

Level I

Belvaspata self-initiations can be done only in conjunction with the use of the alphabet of the Mother Goddess of Creation. *(Fig. 6 on page 36, The Language of the Holy Mother)* In addition, the time periods between periods previously suggested, while the practitioner regularly uses the sigils, must be strictly observed.

The following steps must be taken, in order, for the self-initiation of Level I Belvaspata:

1. Carefully study the material previously written about this healing modality that has come from Mother, including how to heal with Belvaspata.
2. Set aside an 8-hour period to internalize the twelve pairs of emotional frequencies as given previously.
3. Then write out the initiation as given in Mother's language from left to right, from top to bottom, in columns, leaving a space between words. (If more than one page is used per sigil/body location, staple them together.) Each of the three sigils must have its initiation on a separately written page.
4. When complete, place each sigil's drawing on 3 different pages and then on the related body centers with the translation that have been done in Mother's language regarding that sigil.
5. Now read out loud in Mother's tongue what you have written as the initiations. Sign the sigils 3 times in the air.
6. Always end with the sigils for love praise and gratitude, signed by you.

7. Send the original of this translation you have done, with the originals of the 3 sigils you have drawn, to a Belvaspata master of your choice.[21] Request that they issue you a certificate and ask whether they will keep your file to work with issuing your certificates for initiations of Levels II and III as well. This is done so they can ensure observance of the time periods between initiations.

8. If the same master is not available for Levels II and III, send copies of your previous certificates to another, reflecting the dates they were issued.

Level II

Level II self-initiation follows Steps 1 through 8 in Level I, but instead of the 3 sigils, there are nine and the translation for each of these sigil's initiations need to be done, each on a separate page as before.

In preparation for Level II, an 8-hour period needs to be put aside to prepare by internalizing the 16 rays of light instead of the twelve pairs of emotions.

Level III—Mastery

Again, Steps 1 through 8 in Level I are followed. There is only one Master Sigil and only one page of translation (if it runs over onto more than one page, staple them together), but the sigil drawings must be placed 3 times on each of the chakras with the translation one time on each chakra.[22] A day must be set aside in preparation, internalizing love, praise and gratitude.

• By the power of the holy language, I enter into the Level I initiation of Belvaspata.

---

21. See the Belvaspata website for a list.
22. Once the original is done, copies can be used to place on chakras.

- For the opening of my mind, I call in the angel Rutsetviurubach. By the power of his sigil I instruct him to place the sigil of Blautvapata three times in my forehead.
- For the opening of my heart, I call in the angel Iornumubach. By the power of his sigil I instruct him to place the sigil of Kruvechpaururek three times in my heart. (The parts of the ritual that are the same may be copied by hand to make the translation easier)
- For the receptivity of the body, I call in the angel Truararirpleva. By the power of his sigil I instruct him to place the sigil of Kelavisbava three times within my navel. I am now in Level I Belvaspata.

Level II

- By the power of the holy language, I enter into the Level II initiation of Belvaspata. For the release of patterns that no longer serve, I call in the angel Krunechva-atruha. By the power of his sigil I instruct him to place the sigil of Kelavisva-uravech three times in my lower abdomen.
- For the transmuting of matter to energy and then light, I call in the angel Mirakluvael. By the power of his sigil I instruct him to place the sigil of Trechsubareshvi three times in my solar plexus.
- For the transfiguring of illusion to light, I call in the angel Kelevitraunar. By the power of his sigil I instruct him to place the sigil of Patauruhutvi three times in my sternum.
- For the sanctification of the body, I call in the angel Trechbaruruheresvi. By the power of his sigil I instruct him to place the sigil of Kersbaurveshpi three times in my crown.
- For the attracting of light into my voice, I call in the angel

Vilivesbikeresna. By the power of his sigil I instruct him to place the sigil of Kletsutmanarech three times into my throat.

- For the attracting of healing energies into my hands, I call in the angel Kruechnavilshpreva. By the power of his sigil I instruct him to place the sigil of Visbelespahrechvi three times into my right hand.

- For the attracting of healing energies into my hands, I call in the angel Kruechnavilshpreva. By the power of his sigil I instruct him to place the sigil of Visbelespahrechvi three times into my left hand.

- For the DNA activation of the codes of light, I call in the angel Kuuluvet. By the power of his sigil I instruct him to place the sigil of Nenhershbikletrasut 3 times into my root chakra at the base of my spine.

- For the creating of movement in light, I call in the angel Belechhispavatra. By the power of his sigil I instruct him to place the sigil of Veleechsbikluatret 3 times in the alpha chakra. I ask that his wife, Kelipretvaha, place the same sigil in the earth.

- For bringing in the new template of frequency, I call in the angel Kretnauluvesbi. By the power of his sigil I instruct him to place the sigil of Nunmerstararotbelchspi into the bottom of my right foot.

- For bringing in the new template of frequency, I call in the angel Kretnauluvesbi. By the power of his sigil I instruct him to place the sigil of Nunmerstararotbelchspi into the bottom of my left foot.

I am now initiated into Level II of Belvaspata and connected to the planetary grid to bring healing through the use of these sigils. All has become one and one has become all.

Mastery Level

For my initiation into the mastery level of Belvaspata, I call in the angel of the master sigil, Belveresnukvi. By the power of your sigil that I hold, Urhetvi come forth and place this sigil that connects me to the cosmic grid three times in each of the centers I mention.

Place it into the bottom of my left foot and the bottom of my right foot. Place it into my alpha chakra and my root chakra and my lower abdomen. Place it into my navel and my solar plexus and my heart and my sternum. Place it into my throat and my forehead and my crown and my right hand and my left hand. Place it into the tenth chakra ten inches above my crown, known as lahun. Let all become one and one become all. I am now initiated as a master of Belvaspata and am able to initiate others into this sacred healing modality given by the Goddess of Creation.

Additional Information on the Lahun Chakra and its Importance in Mastery

Chakras are energy vortices that act as interfaces between the levels of light in the cosmos and the physical. Light is received by the chakras acting as storage units or capacitors. They then download it to the physical component designed to receive light, at a rate able to be received. The main physical components within the human body are the endocrine glands. However, each cell is also equipped with its own miniscule chakra system. (*Fig. 43, Phase I of Chakra Opening*) (*Fig. 44, Phase II of Chakra Opening*) (*Fig. 45, Phase III of Chakra Opening*)

Phase I of Chakra Opening

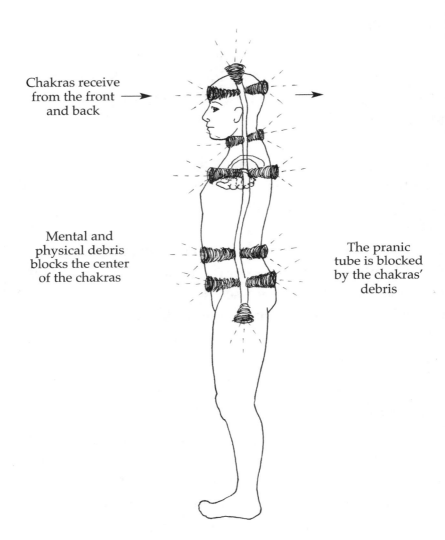

Chakras receive
from the front ⟶
and back

Mental and
physical debris
blocks the center
of the chakras

The pranic
tube is blocked
by the chakras'
debris

Seven levels of light enter the chakras. The light cannot immediately download into the endocrine system because of the blockages of a person who hasn't overcome the past and holds on to that which no longer serves him. The light is assimilated during sleep.

(Figure 43)

Phase II of Chakra Opening

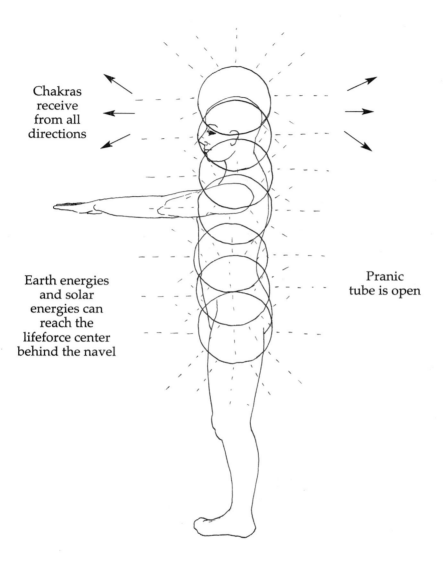

Chakras receive from all directions

Earth energies and solar energies can reach the lifeforce center behind the navel

Pranic tube is open

Less sleep is needed while the endocrine system downloads the seven levels of light. Light is felt as non-cognitive information

(Figure 44)

Phase III of Chakra Opening

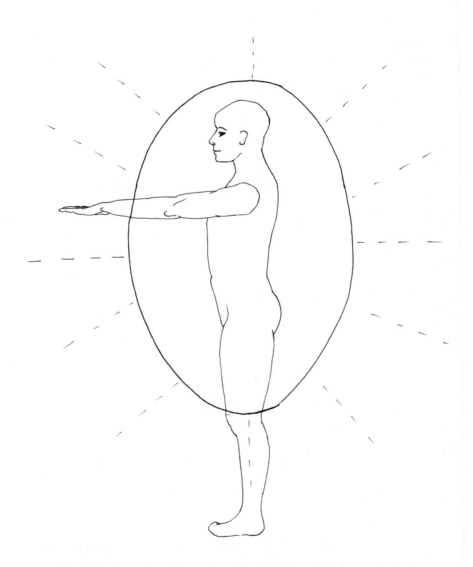

The chakra spheres have opened into a unified chakra field.
The mental body no longer blocks access to light from the higher bodies.

(Figure 45)

The earth too has her chakras, and the opening of the seven seals as described in the Bible (Revelations), refer specifically to the earth's opening of her chakras in preparation for her ascension. Where do these seals or plugs come from?

As trauma or forced change (pain) occurs, there is often a delay in processing the insights the experience yields. In the case of the earth we have to process it for her. The accumulation of these suppressed insights creates a blockage or plug in the center of the chakra. Most people therefore have chakras that are conical to the front and back.

As we start living self-examined lives and extract the insights from past experience, the chakras release their seals and become spherical. The more we become aware of the purpose of indwelling life hiding behind form, the more our chakras open and overlap. Eventually, there is one large unified chakra field. Heartache, sexual stimulation, expanded awareness, and other feelings usually localized within the area of a chakra, now are felt in the entire body.

When the chakra fields unify, a lot more energy is available to the individual and inner guidance becomes strong. The reason for this is that obstruction from the mental body is partially reduced and the influence of the higher bodies floods into the lower bodies. One begins to live in grace; to cooperate with the higher self in living the blueprint for this particular life.

Just prior to entry into God-consciousness, a most miraculous experience transfigures the chakra field yet again. The symbol for this event was depicted by the ancients as a dove, beak pointed upwards, wings extended in a sphere or circle. This signifies the opening of five additional chakras utilized by someone in the second (God-consciousness) and third (Immortal Master) stage (see next section).

The additional five chakras open as a result of incorporating all seven supporting attitudes into our lives. Those attitudes are: Time, Failure, Grace, Poise, Self-Reliance, Reverence and Generosity. Their opening happens in a matter of minutes, unlike the more gradual opening of the other seven. This event may be preceded by physical discomfort and some bruising that comes and goes over major acupuncture points like the wrists.

The experience itself however is blissful and expansive. White light surrounds the body and a violet flame is visible on the head (like the description in the Bible of the flames during Pentecost, visible on the heads of those present). The light has a particular configuration resembling a dove with a circle above its head.

The opening occurs as follows:

1. The areas of the body where a woman's ovaries would be located burst open with white light, first the left, and then immediately the right as chakras eight and nine open;
2. A skirt of light radiates downward, resembling the tail of the dove;
3. This ignites the pranic tube and a great rush of energy travels up from the base of the spine to the crown of the head and the violet flame appears;
4. Immediately afterwards a sphere of light about the size of a dinner plate appears about 8" above the head. It looks like the Sumerian and Egyptian art, depicting the spheres above the heads of those of spiritual power. The tenth chakra is now open;

5. The eleventh chakra in the middle of the right shoulder blade and the twelfth chakra in the middle of the left shoulder blade next open and shoot out wings of light. Angelic beings, who have all twelve chakras open have been portrayed as having wings by those who can see energy directly;

6. The entire configuration of light at this point appears like a dove with a sphere above its head. There is a hidden reason however, why the ancients had the dove enclosed by the circle, rather than having it above the head. The secret lies in the name the Lemurians gave to the number 10 (remember, the circle or sphere above the head is the tenth chakra). The number ten is called "lahun" in Lemurian and some other ancient languages. "La" means all and "hun" means one (la is "all" backwards and languages still have words like "un" or "uno" etc. for one);

The number ten means all in one and one in all (the Atlanteans also knew these secrets behind the law of the one). The sphere above the head will become larger and larger as we progress into the later stages of God-consciousness. At first it will extend all the way to the head, cleaving the flame into two 'horns' on either side (also depicted in ancient art). Eventually, when the Immortal Master overcomes all mortal boundaries, the sphere will enclose all other chakras—all is in one and one is in all.

Such a master now has the vehicle to travel at will with the speed of thought between dimensions and through space and time. The dove is now in the circle. The epitome of what a human being can be has been achieved.

2.11 Questions and Answers About Belvaspata

Q. Does one have to be initiated to use the symbols and if so, how?

A. Absolutely. If one were to ask an initiate, they will be able to describe just how profound the initiation experience is as the symbols are conveyed from a master-healer's hands.

There are two ways to get the initiations: Firstly, there is a Belvaspata website that lists master-healers. If enough students contact a healer to make it worth their while to travel to a specific area, initiations can be performed there.

Secondly, Belvaspata initiations can be done by oneself under the guidance of a master practitioner. Students should prepare by spending a day internalizing the 12 pairs of emotions for level I and the 16 rays of light for level II.

Q. With the new laws of attraction, light attracts opposites. Doesn't this mean light-workers will be surrounded by those in illusion?

A. No, because the Goddess has written into the Book of Life that heart energy will be the most dominant factor in this new cycle, so that opposite energies repel.

Q. Please explain why in the master initiation the chakra 10" above the head is done last and out of order.

A. The Lemurian name for "ten" is "Lahun". This means one in all and all in one. The 'law of the one' the Atlantean mysteries taught about, also pertains to the mystical principles of the 10th chakra:

As an initiate[23] becomes an adept and later a master (all three of these phases are still in Ego-Identification) 12

---

23. See The Stages of Man, 3.1.

chakras open. During subsequent evolutionary stages such as God-Consciousness and ascended mastery, the tenth chakra (about the size of a dinner plate often depicted as a sign of enlightenment above the head in Egyptian and Sumerian art), 10" above the head, enlarges. It continues to grow bigger and bigger until it encloses, all other chakras during the Ascended Mastery stage. All is now in one, and one is in all. By initiating it last, this process is activated.

Q. If we accept payment for this sacred healing modality, aren't we blocking the flow of supply?

A. Every time a first or second level healer uses the symbols, a portion of the earth and its population is healed. Because the master symbol connects the master healer to the cosmic grid, every time a master healer heals with these symbols, it affects the cosmos. How can any amount of money ever be adequate repayment? You will still be leaving the cosmos in debt.

Q. How was this healing modality received by you?

A. I was explaining to a healer in my class in Ireland why her energy based modality wouldn't work, when I saw a group of butterflies come through the windows and turn into symbols as they flew over her right shoulder. They flew into my forehead. I ran to the board and started writing the symbols and accompanying words as rapidly as I could.

Class ended at that point, but in my hotel room, symbols and words and information came through the night until 7am the next morning.

The Ring of White Magic and Power

(also known as the Book of Creation)

3.1 The Book of Creation

Three levels there are for the path you are on
Where you can go depends where you've begun
For some it is perfect to know Level One
This level you write in the Mother's tongue
As all is written, more consciousness comes

II
In Level Two you create what already exists
From a blueprint that is, to a form that persists
When you speak the commands in the language divine
The rose you create won't wither in time

III
When you transcend the human bounds
Then with these words and their holy sound
Create a new form that has never been found

3.2 The Book of Love

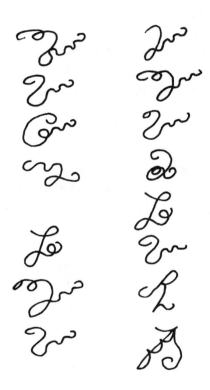

The Sacred Words of Power

I

In the words of the Mother, in her sacred tongue,
That which is, from these words have sprung
Too holy to write, too powerful to keep
This light awakens those who sleep

II

For that which you speak shall surely be
Use them to help and set others free
From the Book of Life these words have come
To banish the darkness, for the dawn has begun

III

The one who wields them must be worthy and true
As they are used, their power accrues
Keep them safe from the profane
They will manifest what you speak on this plane

IV

A space has been left for the name you would use
To speak in the phrase for the one you would choose
To say it but once will work just as well
For their source of power is a bottomless well

V

To you now is passed this mantle of light
Speak from the heart to create what is right
The face of the Goddess shines through these words
To banish illusion wherever they're heard

VI

Magic, you say, but really not so
For magic's results will come and go
But this eternal, you should know,
As the Source of power from which it flows

(Translation of the Sacred Words)

Bel sutvra Erkluch Trauna

I

Peresh perukvi, Ama sut perenu
Kef ura virablish pel uvra nu
Sparu tre vach var ba, uhurespi klavet
Spu uva tra vuna, pel uvravet

II

Kliush utraviva kliuch paruna
Pel uvra uvefir bish kla utrasa
Velech peruchvi uruvish u trave
Nin hurt sparachvi uba klesh trauva

III

Peres pra nuchvi pelevich uvastraa
Kre-unach uvra uvreshbi tre mispataa
Keluch ubra sutravi kelesh balaa
Verch uvra heresvi kluch uf vataa

IV

Kresut mich natvich beleuch nun trave
Kres u bra uvrasut nin ursh barkle
Elech pre nun harvet speurach nunklavaa
Belesh bri eravich nun hersh pataa

V

Pla pluf nun trahurg urevespi travaa
Krech urna manavech spurat plavaa
Kersh krug nun verhat travaa Ma-ur travaa
Speurich un traveshpavi eruch skarnet,
Pelsh espa uravit kels usabaa

VI

Trauch pare uruvespi palesh
Nen hurt urklabish treus travesh
Setlu paretvi urukletvi pare
Pel uvra kletrubik nun pelechve

3.3 The Book of Awareness

Also Known as the Book of White Magic

The following you read
No translation you need
For it's written in gold
unseen and untold

In Mother's tongue in words unseen
Angels echo the words you mean
Filled with power, they're sacred and true
What you speak is what you do

A gift from the Mother they surely are
To the ones She has gathered from near and far
To restore the balance of power and light
To heal and uplift, to do what is right

White magic they are, newly restored
Hidden from cycles of darkness before
They're given this day, both ancient and new
Create through the heart and they'll work for you

So simple they seem but they're not as they appear
They're far more than they seem it must be clear
Speak exactly the way they're written for you
The words are of power and they will come true

Statements to Speak

Magic so pure is brought now to man
In the Book of Life, in a gold-dipped pen
Recorded they are; this you must know
So that when you speak it makes it so

Statements

1. Businesses are a blessing to all connected with them in any way, producing the best products and services possible.

2. All are able to go within to get all the guidance needed from the Goddess.

3. It is now possible for every living being to reach their highest potential.

4. All now have all the free education they need to do all they are here to do, and more.

5. Education is balanced between thinking, feeling, learning, doing and seeing with inner guidance and love.

6. Education is balanced between inner expression and outer expression for the good of all.

7. The homes of all are useful, beautiful, spacious and supportive to the lives of the inhabitants: they are lived in with love, wisdom and power.

8. There is peace and love exchanged between the human and animal kingdoms.

9. All are encouraged to share their wisdom, power, knowledge and love with others who will appreciate it.

10. There are games that challenge and delight every being and help them grow in every way.

11. All unlock the secrets of the universe and use them wisely for good.

12. Travel is available to all who wish to visit and learn from other worlds and dimensions.

13. All are able to see a measure of the Goddess' beauty in all that surrounds them.

14. The secrets of organic life are being unlocked to bring great wisdom, knowledge and understanding to those who are ready.

15. There are schools to teach levels of perception to all who are ready to learn.

16. All are able to telepathically communicate with one another and animals when desired.

17. There is free energy available for the individual and collective use of all.

18. All have ideal foods that are delicious, healthy and life-enhancing.

19. Ascension is made easy for those who are ready.

20. All have opportunities to share their gifts, abilities, talents and lives with others.

21. The waters are pristine and clear.

22. The atmosphere of the earth is maintained in a condition that is healthy for all life.

23. The land of the earth is cared for and maintained in a way that is ideal to produce fertility and sustainability for all life.

24. Beings of love, light and mastery are always available to teach, remove the illusion of disease and instruct all who desire it.

25. The vibrations over the surface of the earth are periodically raised to a higher level of love, light and joy as the beings in each area are ready for it.

26. All have work that brings joy, growth and attainment.

27. All on earth teach that which they have learned to those who wish to know.

28. Everyone has access to travel that is free and joyful.

29. Each female of the cosmos holds in highest esteem her power, strength, beauty, nurturing love, sensuality, wisdom and oneness with all Creation as it resides within.

30. All females' words of wisdom are revered throughout the cosmos.

31. All females reflect the pure essence of the divine Mother.

32. The clear choice of life is what is life-enhancing. Let all focus on it.

33. All are one.

34. Forgiveness is the key that turns on the light within.

35. Be the cause that knows there is nothing separate.

36. Love yourself while loving the Goddess with all your heart, mind and strength.

37. May the Spirit of Mother transmute every mis-thought and mis-perception.

38. See the reflection of Mother in all and know your divinity.

39. Let go and be peace.

40. The Goddess is perfect love—let all nature reflect this.

41. Effortless knowing occurs within the silence of the mind.

42. I am all that I am here and now, ascended and immortal.

43. We are all whole in our oneness, now.

44. There is only love and the other pure emotions.

45. May others become enlightened as I do.

46. All life is appreciated.

47. Children are born with their hearts open wide, with awareness of and trust in mother's love.

48. All life prospers and blooms with love.

49. All kingdoms and realms live in harmony with diversity, and in support of each other.

50. All life knows and loves Mother and reflects her perfection every day in every way.

51. All sense and live the magic in their lives every moment.

52. Every feeling, thought or act of love, praise and gratitude increases the same attitude in ourselves and others.

53. Mother's love streams through our hearts.

54. In unity and with joy, all beings evolve with kindness, gentleness and unconditional love and light.

55. Lightness of being uplifts us and makes us aware of our highest identity as a being as vast as the cosmos.

56 Our light shines effortlessly, as does our love flow effortlessly like rivers.

57. We are free to express our fullest potential.

58. We know all that we are.

59. We live in the moment, expressing the fullness of love in every form.

60. The love in our hearts enables us to see clearly and know our truth.

61. All beings awaken from the dream of identity.

62. Love is lived within the heart of every being.

63. We know we are the love of the universe.

64. We sing with joy.

65. We live our highest truth within every moment.

66. Like souls come together, creating families of light.

67. A deep, loving recognition is felt for others of like energy.

68. We know we are the One being mirrored many times.

69. Illusion falls away this moment, without even an echo remaining.

70. Love moves through every aspect of our being.

71. All beings live in awakened awareness.

72. Universal love flows freely throughout the cosmos.

73. Mother bestows grace and abundance in the hearts of all children.

74. All children know and feel the love and mercy that encompasses all Creation.

75. All hearts are comforted.

76. All children have inspiration, support and love.

77. All have an environment of love in which to express.

78. Fathers give enduring support and nurturance to mothers and children.

79. Children are taught to love all life, enabling them to experience other dimensions.

80. Earth expands in an infinite glory of light and love that vibrates throughout all Creation.

81. All children receive guidance through love.

82. Children respect and love their parents.

83. There is a revelation of the Mother's infinite light, brighter than the heavens have ever known.

84. All children are parented with the same support and nurturing Mother gives all Creation.

85. Parenting is regarded as a privilege and honor by all.

86. Children know and express their creative gifts.

87. The rays of love, praise and gratitude permeate all thought.

88. All express all pure emotions and rays of light embodied by Mother.

89. Relationships with animals as companions are established by mutual consent.

90. All beings are innocent as they dance through life.

91. All beings feel at home and welcome wherever they are.

92. All are aware of the inter-connectedness of life.

93. All feel free to manifest their hearts' purest desires.

94. Only life-enhancing words and energies are expressed.

95. The sacred city of light takes form for all to see.

96. The Mother is consciously known and revered by every being.

97. Mother's public reign of the cosmos from earth begins.

98. Angels and other beings of light are visible to all.

99. Miracles abound to uplift all.

100. To the Mother forever give all glory.

A hundred affirmations I give you
Their sacredness known but to a few
The profane will see them as worthy of naught
But you alone will know their import
Say them in service, say them aright
Through them you spread your love and your light.

Pelech vi nusbi, pelech vi-rar
Yelshpi va truanok, urvi blanadar
Bers pranu ui-nak, urvastana vabir
Kel ura nureshpi, klanug varahir

Trenuch palespi, uhurut manadoch
Bel uvra uvrestra, uret panaroch
Mir abel stravi, kelenustra struvaa
Besh uvi hech spavi, kel-nun-hustaar

Granoch paleski uhuret parnavaa
Tre urva dananoch uret nun hervaa
Uruhesh nun her trevabi, skleruski paranut
Yel-kek vra uvraset, pelech vra spaurut

3.4 The Book of Light

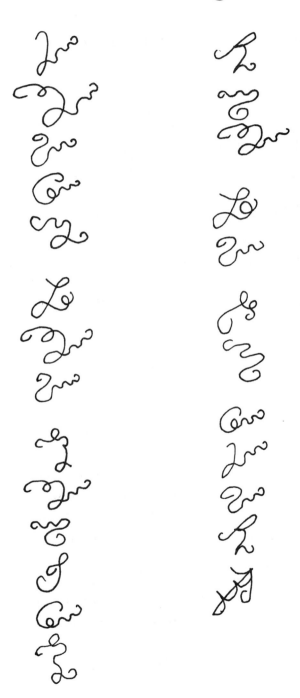

3.5 Pronunciation of Mother's Language

The pronunciation is very much like German, other than that the 'v' (as in very) and 'w' (as in white) are pronounced as in English.

The syllables are pronounced individually when placed next to each other. There are no contracted sounds like 'au' (as in trauma). It would be necessary to say the 'a' and 'u' separately. The only exception to this rule is a double 'aa' at the end of a word. This indicates a long 'a' sound (as in spa).

The 'ch' spelling at the **beginning** of a word is the only time it is pronounced as in 'church'. Everywhere else it is pronounced as in the German 'kirche' or somewhat like the Spanish x as in Mexico.

- 'u' is pronounced as in 'prudence'.
- 'a' is pronounced as in 'Barton'.
- 'e' is as in 'pet'.
- 'i' is pronounced as in 'pink'.
- 'o' is pronounced in the was someone with an English accent would say 'of' or 'cross'.
- 'g' is always a hard 'g' like 'great'.
- 'c' is always hard as in 'call'.
- 'q' has a 'qw' sound as in 'queen'.
- 'r' is slightly rolled—'rr'.
- 'y' is pronounced as in 'Yvette', with an 'ee' sound.

There are many words for 'I' or 'is' because of frequency changes. "I am happy" has a much higher frequency than "I am tired", and "I" or "am" would therefore be different in each of these sentences.

Also, when the concept is large, several words are needed. 'Beautiful' will have different words depending on what is described, but in each case the term will have several words since it is a complex concept.

There are no words for 'sad', 'pain', 'angry', 'protective' or 'fear', since those are illusory concepts in this creation of life. There are also no negative words.

'I' and 'we' would be the same word as this is a group consciousness language. Similarly, 'he' and 'they' would use the same word.

SECTION FOUR

The Ring of Spiritual Warriorship

4.1 Changing a Million Years of Toltec Tradition

The Toltec tradition was designed to not only map the way through the unknown, but also to utilize it as a growth mechanism. It originated directly from Mother to help preserve the masculine grid in all its integrity.

She knew that power-mongers would attempt to disrupt these grids (lines of light that tell groups of beings how to live) and the information that flows along them. For this reason the Toltec way was given as the impeccable way to work with power. It provided a way to harness energy and increase perception by turning the unknown into the known through experience.

In the summer of 2006, after a year and a half of cosmic ascension which saw the cosmos move through higher and higher frequency bands, the unknown was successfully turned into the known. What had been the primary purpose of the Toltec path no longer existed—nine-tenths of its tenets and philosophy became obsolete as the unknown ceased to be.

The external source of power and perception (external opposition) had necessitated an external form of warriorship which was masculine in nature and was therefore part of the masculine grid. The new form of warriorship is internal, since there is nothing external to protect against, nor are there exterior portions of the unkown. Because the new creation studies the known, the unknown has taken on a new meaning; it now tells us how the known should be applied and expanded. This is why the Toltec way has to be re-written as we study the new feminine warriorship.

The Toltec Practices

Toltec practices used in everyday life to develop the tools of discernment were based on the four directions. As the directions themselves have reversed in nature, so too the practices and tools the Toltecs need have altered:

1. Combing the Shadows

This practice is similar to scanning a landscape, except you are scanning the landscape of your life. The goal is to find any areas creating a tension of some sort in your body or emotions. If your stomach feels like 'a knot' when you are at work, the next thing to determine is the cause.

2. Cultivating Mindlessness

You comb the individuals at your work, using the process of asking questions and obtaining symbols, as described in The New Process of Discernment in Section 1. Cultivating mindlessness gives you the ability to quickly access the symbols you need. If combing the individuals does not show you what produces the stress, go through each of your projects or work areas. It may be a location where something could fall on you, in which case the symbol may be a hammer or a weight of some sort. When you cannot narrow it down any further, ask for another symbol, and so on.

Fear of failure brings thought into our work. The truth is, however, that mindlessness and automatic work produce fewer errors. It is the warrior's new way to stretch mindlessness further and further into all areas of his or her life.

3. Developing Your Symbolic Language[24]

Let us suppose you want to know why there's a tightening in your stomach when you are around the boss at work. The image might be a red flag, which means 'danger'. You ask "Is my job in danger?" Then you may see a fish, which means "no". If you see a repeat of the red flag, it means yes. If you ask whether your boss is in danger of losing his job, you again will get a symbol for a yes or a no.

A good place to start cultivating this language of symbols is to learn the symbol that will be used for your yes or no. It may be a circle for yes and a circle with a line through for no. The symbols will be specific for you: a red hand may mean you've caught someone red-handed. A nut-cracker may mean you've cracked the nut, or solved the problem. If you don't understand the symbol, ask for another. Become familiar with a body of symbols and use common sense. (See Appendix I) **Feel** what the symbol represents to you at that moment.

4. Pulsing the Emotions

The goal of perception through the cultivation of the tools of discernment is the stimulating of the new 12 pairs of emotions. The expanse and clarity of the images received will increase as the negative and positive aspects of the emotions pulse more strongly.

24. See Appendix I

The Tools of Discernment

The more the four practices are incorporated into life, the greater the skill at wielding the tools of discernment. Working and thinking with the emptiness of mind should become a way of life.

Not only do the symbols on the inner screen of our minds speak to us, but so does everything in our environment. Failure to understand its language is the most aggravated form of illiteracy. All of our book learning doesn't compensate for being illiterate when it comes to reading life.

1. Feeling the tension within the bodies (South)

Sweating, nausea, a tight throat or stomach, itchy spots—all these signal that something needs to be examined. Using the tools we've been given, we identify a problem. Let's say it is connected with our job. What do we do in a situation where we have uncovered that our boss intends to fire us?

First, we must remember how our bodies feel when we're at work. Do we feel wonderfully at peace and at home? If not, our boss may just be one step ahead of us in the sorting process where opposite energies now repel. We may want to immediately send out resumes and quit before we're fired.

If we love our work and everyone there and feel at home in the environment, we may want to sit down with the boss to ask how we can make ourselves indispensable. We then re-create our job accordingly.

In order to take in the responses of our bodies and emotions, we slow our pace a bit and use extra time to receive guidance through our symbols. The physical responses are a gift of this Creation–they will definitely be guiding you now, even if they

166

didn't before.

2. Imaging Symbols (West)

The best way to begin using this gift is to initially work in pairs. One asks the question, while the other gets the images. Although we must be able to do both functions ourselves, this allows us a familiarity with the symbols and the process. No analysis should be done until after the process is complete in terms of the ultimate message of the symbols. If you are the one asking the questions, do just enough silent deduction to direct the questions where the symbols lead.

The one whose turn it is to get the images speaks about nothing else, keeping the screen of his mind blank. Even if you are talented at getting information in other psychic ways, don't use them. This is not just an alternative way to receive information, it is the new way of thinking.

3. Interpreting the Symbols (East)

Up to this point, the information is going to be fully dependable. Make absolutely sure that your interpretation is equally unbiased by double-checking the responses. If you got a white ribbon when you asked if someone was guilty of something, ask "Does this stand for innocence?" If you see the ribbon again, you've interpreted it correctly.

An example of how we interpret meaning according to what we want it to be occurred in one of my classes. A young man wanted to know whether to move to Arizona or not. The person he was working with saw a mule-train in a canyon surrounded by red rocks reminiscent of the Southwest area. The young man interpreted it to mean that because the wagon was heavily laden, that he had a lot of supplies and was well prepared. He thought the high rock walls of the canyon meant it was safe.

Because he did not want to hear the truth, I did not bother to explain that a vehicle traveling by land means a change in general awareness. The fact that it was an ox-drawn wagon versus a train meant that change (which is why he wanted to go), would come in a slow burdensome way. He would be bringing his old baggage with him, impeding progress. The rock walls on either side of him indicated he had narrow vision about the whole move.

4. Discerning whether action or change is needed (North)

It is from this wonderful inner guidance system that our life strategies are formed. In determining what changes are needed and how to implement them, emotions become our guiding light. The practice of pulsing our emotions has made us very sensitive to their presence. The ripple of joy or the whisper of inspiration will tell us which change is best and most life-enhancing. In this way our plans come from our inner core, our most authentic parts, and we create our future through the heart.

The more we incorporate the four practices into our life, the greater our skill in wielding the tools of discernment. Working and thinking with emptiness of mind should become a way of life.

4.2 Changes in the Toltec Way

The Toltec was a warrior against illusion, which no longer exists. The word Toltec comes from the Lemurian word Ta-al-taka, meaning 'practitioner of inclusiveness'. In addition to the duty of assisting others remove illusion and obtain freedom, the Toltec Naguals practiced inclusiveness. They feel very much at home in the new creation where inclusiveness is the only way of life that will flourish.

What is inclusiveness?

• Inclusiveness acts from one's highest identity. Every interaction and decision originates from this vantage point.

• It considers the effects on all life that every action will have. It helps us know that we are each the center of our cosmos, exerting the most profound influence on all life with our smallest action.

• Inclusiveness knows that to benefit the whole is to benefit ourselves. It acknowledges the oneness of all life.

• It changes the external mirrors by changing ourselves within. Now that all externally reflects what Mother is, any lingering illusion must be coming from within.

Changes Within the Toltec Teachings

The teachings accomplished what they set out to do; lead us to freedom. Now only 10% of them are still applicable. There is no more unknown as it applies to illusion. The unknown now concerns new and unknown ways to apply the known. The threats associated with the illusion we faced before have disappeared.

1. The Warrior's Shield

Although the emotion of protectiveness is now obsolete, the first part of the warrior's shield has to do with safeguarding his wellbeing. He (or she) must remind himself that appearances are not what they seem, and move forward with the utmost awareness. He must be alert to the guidance of his bodily responses to that which he encounters. Because his wellbeing is guarded for him by the new cosmic laws that cause opposite energies to repel, he just has to pay attention. Is he nauseated in someone's presence? Do his muscles tense, his throat constrict? He needs to remove himself from any situation that constricts his life. He is always to act from the most authentic of the twelve emotional pairs. In the previous cycle, perception was the primary guidance but now the new emotions are.

2. The Premises of Problem Solving

Rather than using mind to identify the source of a problem and to explore ways to resolve it, we now ask our hearts for a solution that would apply at least one of the pairs of twelve true emotions, benefiting all concerned. We remind ourselves we can create what we love; there is no set plan we have to abide by.

- We remember that we are reflecting the true nature of the Infinite Mother; that all decisions need to reflect the perfect compassion of her Being.

- We carefully note the responses of our emotions and body to portions of the problem before us. They tell us which portions and people have opposite energies. Accept as valid the desire to repel portions of the information being presented.

- We remind ourselves that the highest service we can render to all life is to live in a way that makes our hearts sing and evokes genuine emotions. We further remind ourselves that this is the new form of compassion; that to hold on to that which is being repelled from within, or is repelling us from without, serves no one. Sometimes those of opposite energy may recognize the need to repel us before we do.

The Warrior's Code

With energy in limitless supply as one of the rays of light, and that which is depleting automatically repels, the warrior no longer has to conserve energy or organize his life around frugality, the need to compress time or to maintain constant alertness against the possibility of having to make a last stand. He no longer focuses on details, instead surrendering to the moment and discarding his sense of individual identity. He knows he is not his experiences.

The warrior accesses energy through the ascension attitudes, bringing love, praise and gratitude to every moment so he can draw on the endless supply of awareness and energy. In lavish expression of the new emotions, he surrounds himself with that which promotes love, praise and gratitude and repels that which does not. As long as the emotional pairs pulse each other, the new emotions can be lived as abundantly as possible.

Now that time is obsolete, the new guideline tells us that because there is only this moment, all other moments are contained within it. We change ourselves in the present moment.

Those who have earned the right to participate in this creation have already successfully made their last stand. Interacting sparingly or not at all with those of opposite energy, we are prepared every moment to find that which delights us. We no longer need to prepare for the worst to earn the luxury to expect the best. That which will delight us is in front of us at all times.

Because the moment is all there is, we focus on the moment. This creation is designed for creativity and fun as we explore our being and what brings us joy. The more joy we have, the more we grow. We are therefore constantly changing. Getting to know ourselves is a never-ending process, done moment by moment. The crucial part is to never get stuck in a rut—this will slow growth almost to a standstill. Embracing the new will help expand us and that is growth. The goal, therefore, is to embrace the newness of ourselves in every moment and to welcome new experiences that make our hearts sing.

We are guided by our instinct at all times, slowing our lives and being guided by our body truth. There is no more urgency to become, just the joy of being.

The guiding rule of living without identity is one that deals with that which is. It doesn't change from its former purpose. We are still in reality as a unique perspective as vast as the cosmos. We still strenuously resist identifying with our experiences or the roles we are playing.

Summary of the New Warrior's Codes

- The warrior abundantly surrounds himself with that which promotes love, praise and gratitude and repels that which doesn't.
- Because there is only this moment, all other moments are contained within it. We change ourselves in the present. We seek that which will delight us in every moment and remove ourselves from that which does not.
- We explore ourselves through that which we love and our heart's desires. It is an endless journey for we are new every moment.
- We slow our lives in order to have our instincts and body truth guide us.
- We have no identity and can play any role we choose. We are not our experiences.

Understanding the Instinctual Self

In the previous creation, the instinctual nature was the first to pick up and interpret the potential that lay outside the being;

another line of evolution, like the God-kingdom, for example. The feminine instinctual part interpreted the potential through action or art while the masculine held the space or boundaries, pushing them out as far as possible.

Because the roles reversed, the potential to be explored is now the inner one, which finds that which has never before been delved into. It may just be a feeling, but now the male instinctual self acts it out with wild abandonment. As he inspires the feminine (which is now holding the space) into responding emotionally, she expands and expands the arena in which his interpretation takes place, enabling him to express even more.

4.3 Concepts in the New Creation

What is Warriorship?

Previously we had to pierce illusion to find its insight. Now illusion has been completely solved. The warrior now ignores illusion since it no longer belongs to the Infinite (just held onto by individuals), finding that which is true and beautiful and reflects the Infinite each moment.

What is Truth?

Linear guidelines of conduct, such as justice, no longer exist; we no longer have to seek these truths. Truth is what we masterfully create moment by moment through the heart. We stand before a blank canvas, paintbrush in hand; there are no 'paint by number' guidelines called 'truth'. Instead, truth is what we will make of it moment by glorious moment.

What is Perception?[25]

Perception is noticing our innocence and beauty in outside

25. For more in-depth explanation, see the section in Perception, Power and Energy at the end of The Ring of Spiritual Warriorship.

mirrors. Feeling with non-cognitive perception the specific nuance or flavor the mirror brings to the familiar portions of ourselves, allows us to expand to include it. This makes that which we are deeper and richer.

What is Challenge?

Challenge is the utmost test of fluidity, the hallmark of a warrior of light. Previously held patterns associated with illusion, and the beings created to represent it, have become obsolete overnight. All beings alive have been re-created to mirror the pristine impeccability of the Mother. We are to see illusion as the remaining wisps of smoke after the fire is long since dead.

What is the Purpose of Existence?

The new purpose of existence is to create through the heart; to see just how many ways we can find to mirror Mother's face—her joy, abundance, generosity and devotion to the pure in heart. Nature has mirrored much of it; now it is time for our lives to do the same.

What is the Known?

The known has not changed. It was and is those portions of the One Being, the Infinite Mother, that have been turned into something familiar through experience. It is light and reflects that which She is. To see the good in each moment, we have to have it in ourselves. We can only recognize what is within us. We are therefore observing in various nuances our own being by finding what we love in our environment.

What is the Unknown?

The one-tenth of creation that remains unknown doesn't in any way represent illusion, but rather the creative application of the known. We use the fragments of illusion clung to by those in this material life, as an energy source and focus instead on just how much diversity of expression we can bring to that which is part of the 12 pure emotional pairs.

What is Intent?[26]

Although intent is still the moving force of the cosmos that clusters awareness into form, the process of how it's done has changed. Every soul that exists has been re-formed into the higher perfection of what Mother is, which is purity, light and love. As we see something in our environment that inspires us with love, praise and gratitude it is because that something already exists within us—something of purity, light and love,

In the new creation, it is only possible to create through focused pure emotions and attitudes of love, praise and gratitude. It is therefore impossible to create further chaos. Any apparent remaining chaos is only a remnant of illusion some insist on keeping a while longer. It cannot linger indefinitely. But new chaos as an actual creation that has 'real' substance or indwelling life, cannot be formed. Such intent will no longer successfully create results.

What is the Silence of the Mind?

The external warriorship in the preceding cycles characterized by illusion (there were 9 of these cycles, each trillions of years long—called *Hurplesplek-urnavestresh-abruhelesvi-klauvachvra-kreunit*) dictated that a warrior against illusion live by challenge. To keep his objectivity and access through feeling what lay behind appearances, he cultivated silence of the mind. Because those nine cycles themselves consisted of separation consciousness designed to study illusion, silence of the mind

26. The next section further explains changes in Intent.

was hard to achieve.

When the inner dialog has ceased, the assemblage point moves freely. This allows us to easily move in and out of altered states and view prospective choices from all angles.

What is the Riddle of the Heart?

Previously, the riddle was the understanding of the nature of reality as a series of holographic scenes that a Toltec had the ability to access at will by shifting his assemblage point. In previous creations, separate worlds existed like a set of boxes stacked on top of each other and a warrior could leave this one at will and visit another.

The warrior was able to walk the path of power after conceptually and experientially mastering the art of stalking, the mastery of awareness and the mastery of intent. However he had to understand the riddle of the heart before he could utilize the art of stalking.

The art of stalking can be defined as the deliberate shifting of the perspective in which the warrior lives, to allow him to view his experiences objectively, to determine the impeccable choices of action, and to eliminate social conditioning as the determining factor in his decision making. This art has not changed in the new creation, as it pertains to the known.

The riddle of the heart has changed somewhat. Now the 'boxes' aren't stacked on top of one another but are rather nested inside one another; and the assemblage point opens the walls between them. They physical and etheric realms have merged—it's no longer a matter of leaving one to enter another. Now the assemblage point position determines how many of these realms we can see superimposed over this one at once. Each has become a permanent part of every other reality and will no longer disassemble or 'go away' just because we are also accessing another.

The riddle of the mind occurs in that portion of the warrior's journey called the 'mastery of awareness'. It is the result of his encounter with the vastness that is the extent of man's awareness. As a consciousness superimposed over all that is, the warrior finds his true identity as something that never ends and the body simply a reference point within it. This has not changed other than that the vastness that is man has lost any deliberate areas of distortion that had enabled him to study the unknown, which can now be studied in its clarity—a study that never ends.

What is the Riddle of the Spirit Now?

The third area of experiential knowledge cultivated by the Toltec was and is the manipulation of reality through intent (the definition of magic). Man has always been a magical being of the cosmos, affecting all life; he just has not fully understood how much. The riddle of the spirit presented itself when he did try to explore the extent of his influence within the cosmos and found that the cosmos itself is just a box within a box, etc., that never ends. Within this vastness, his influence doesn't end either. The body is not only a point of reference within this vastness but also a fulcrum point upon whose life everything pivots.

The Infinite Mother has explained a miniscule portion of this to me as follows:

1. The cosmos is one of trillions of cells in a larger body.
2. This larger body is one of 144,000 bodies within each other (just as our physical, etheric, emotional, mental bodies, etc.

stack inside one another like Russian dolls).

3. Mother has taken on a physical form here on earth. These 144,000 bodies are simply a reflection of the information held in one of the trillions of cells of her body.

4. This cosmos is but a drop in a never-ending ocean.

What is the Art of Dreaming?

In Appendix V to this book we discuss with the Master Horlet the new way of working. We also saw that the same method applied to interpreting the promptings of the heart as the mind is emptied and symbols flit across its empty screen. These symbols are then interpreted as shown in Appendix I. Previously, the warrior used dreaming as a tool from time to time. Now he lives within it at all times. A new form of thinking has replaced linear thought.

What is the Way of Encountering the Unknown?

Previously, as lightseekers were attracting opposite energies, they needed a great deal of protectiveness and strategy when encountering the unknown. Now that life's new laws of opposite energies repel, we embark on a journey to discover that which is, with the twelve pairs of emotions the only tools required. If an encounter with an unknown produces the desire to discover why something inside us resonates with it, that is a clear indication that we should explore it.

Knowing that the core of everything is re-formed into purity, we either find the energy of it inspirational and life-enhancing or we don't and move away. Because we no longer view opposite-energy events as our sources of power and perception, we are only interested in finding those things and people that inspire us to expand.

Fluidity

The average person sees the nature of reality as static or fixed. Life to him is like a maze through which he somehow has to find his way, using the concept of truth as a guide. This is why many are so dogmatic, or even fanatic, about their belief systems of what is true and what is not.

The spiritual warrior of the Toltec sees life as fluid. He knows that any belief system will put him in a cage while the fluid river of life flows by him. He strives to cultivate a life of no expectations, and instead of trying to understand the aspects of change that arise before him moment by moment, he simply cooperates with them. This perfect fluidity prevents him from falling prey to the addiction many have of needing to know or understand that which is born from fear of the unknown.

The warrior doesn't seek truth or understanding, only the clarity to know the next step in his fluid cooperation with life. Truth is not absolute in that it describes a set of rules to follow. In its broadest sense, truth is that which reflects the nature of the Infinite. The warrior knows that, as a facet of the Infinite, he is created from the very fabric of truth. Truth is what he brings forth from the authentic core of his being.

He does not search for meaning, because from his vantage point, he cannot understand the vast moving forces that can be grasped only by the Infinite. To attempt to do so would be to assign labels to the unknowable, trapping him into taking life at face value.

But by following his heart as it responds in the stillness of his mind to the ever-changing current of life, he watches only for his next step. He watches for clarity in how to respond and contribute to the fluid unfolding of the universe. He knows that he need not understand, but only cooperate, because understanding requires a fixed frame of reference which is not available in a cosmos where every thought changes the direction of the river.

Social Conditioning

The programming inflicted on beings from birth is the greatest bondage in existence. It dictates how life should be lived and tries to put life into labeled boxes, reducing the great adventure of the discovery of self to mediocrity and boredom.

Social conditioning is the attempt by man to hold onto what he thinks of as sanity. He fears he might lose all frame of reference to his own identity within the vastness of existence. To let go of all social conditioning will eliminate identity. But it is not the loss of identity that is madness, but having identity in the first place.

When we let go of our conditioned identity, we find the expansiveness of our awareness. Within this expanse, we play many roles. Identifying with any of them is to attempt to put the ocean in a bucket.

To avoid social conditioning, the warrior questions everything and observes the origin of his every decision and action. In this way he sees whether they originate from the authentic wellspring of his soul or from the fixation on a worldview imposed by others.

The Path of Knowledge

In previous creations, blind spots of untruth were encoded into our DNA, forcing us to find truth 'outside' ourselves by studying it in the mirrors of our environment. We then internalized it by turning it into experience. This process turned the quest for knowledge into a struggle.

Those blind spots were removed for every being when we entered this creation. Everyone now reflects the innocence and purity of the Creational Mother's being. We no longer have to wrestle with the exterior circumstances of our lives to find the truth.

The knowledge we have sought has always been the knowledge of our own being. That has not changed. It is no longer obscured, but is readily available through the heart. Knowledge gained without is no longer internalized through experience. Instead, the inner knowledge flows through our hearts as a knowingness to be externalized without as experience. The direction of the flow of knowledge has reversed.

There is no longer anything standing in the way of our gaining all knowledge in an ever-expanding capacity. Our attitudes are the silences that allow the bountiful stream of knowledge of the Mother to flow through us. The knowledge of the Infinite is held in the perception aspect of awareness. Awareness in turn responds to love, praise and gratitude.

Knowledge therefore flows to us through these attitudes and is felt through the unique lens of our individual heart. When it is externalized by our living experientially our heart's desires, we study in each other (remember, others of like energy are now entering our environment) that which we are.

The process of gaining knowledge has become painless, easy and quick.

Intelligent Cooperation with Life

With no separation between the etheric, or indwelling life aspect of our existence, we have merged with our higher selves.

Toltecs called this the intelligent cooperation with life. Matter has become spiritualized. It has become 'real'. There isn't a higher self any more as we knew it, nor is there a script or destiny to follow. Where, then, does our guidance come from and what is there to cooperate with to live and create our highest truth?

We have eliminated the need to go through the 'middle man' of our higher aspect to receive information from our highest self—the individuated awareness that spans all of existence. We have joined forces with that higher self and now receive directly from our highest self the pure emotions of the Infinite, the Creational Mother's desire to know that which she is. This comes to us as desire through our hearts. Now the path of listening to the promptings of what makes our hearts sing is all we need to live at our highest level.

The Madness within the Dream

The madness within the dream was a term used to describe the fact that we (as our higher self) designed our experiences for our highest good, then felt victimized by them. We designed our life's experiences down to the minutest details and agreed to embody them, then we prayed to be 'saved' from their unpleasantness.

The madness now has a different form; that of a hypochondriac. Even though we may have been 'diseased' as a cosmic experience and have had discordant energies within us, that is over.

Since time has collapsed, even the memory of discordance has been erased. In addition, because Mother re-formed us, re-creating us in the perfection of her Being, the disease does not exist any more. Protectiveness, anger, pain and fear are all remnants of that past 'disease'. The war games of nations, the struggle for supremacy are there only because some still hold them in place like hypochondriacs. Glance at them if you must, but do not give illusion power by allowing it to affect you in any way; that would be the madness within the dream.

What is the Unknowable?

The unknowable is that which has not yet been developed. Subtle whisperings run through every soul, hinting of things that still lie dormant as potential. Before, the heart whispered of that which lay without, beckoning for us to become. The direction of within was the vehicle of that which lay without and could be achieved. Then the direction of flow reversed. Now the direction of Within whispers of things yet unborn within the depth of our soul. As we develop these potentials, Mother does also, since we are representatives of what she is. When Mother grows, all life benefits.

What is the Assemblage Point?

(See Fig. 3, page 16, The Seven Bodies of Man)

Whereas the assemblage point has always been on the outer edge of the bodies of man, the new creation has it placed deeper into his luminous cocoon. The reason is that in April 2005 the earth moved out of its position in space and began pulling all of the cosmos behind it. The Mother of All Creation took up her position here on earth; and the earth became the cosmic assemblage point.

Before, the earth was on the edge of the cosmos pulling us deeper into what was then the unknown (a fact obscured by a hologram kept around the earth) it is now stationary and will instead have star-systems arrange themselves around us. Eighty percent of the Antares star system will be the first. Thus when the hologram is removed, the 'new heavens' Christ speaks about it Revelations will be visible.

The earth, as the cosmic assemblage point, will have moved deeper into the body of the cosmos. The assemblage point of man will do likewise.

What is Death?

Toltec seers described death as a tumbling force. They knew that there was some powerful grinding force pummeling the luminous cocoon of man, but they were unable to identify this force because, until January 5, 2005, the third form of awareness had not been discovered. *(Fig. 4, on page 24, The Three Types of Awareness)*

Seers knew that trillions of spiraling rays of awareness were radiating forth from some inconceivably powerful Source. But the fact that they also arced, eluded them. It is this movement, however, that caused the grinding force against the bodies of man. The Tumbler was nothing more than the movement of awareness.

This 'tumbling' of the luminous cocoon of man caused wear and tear, which leaked energy and in turn caused aging. Eventually, when enough energy had leaked out, the cocoon could no longer withstand the tumbling forces, cracked and crumpled in upon itself. The more life was resisted, the more the wear and tear on the cocoon.

But there were a few rare individuals called 'saints' (from the Lemurian word 'San', meaning one who cooperated with the serpents of heaven, or spirals of awareness), who managed to thwart death. Instead of resisting these trillions of spiraling, grinding rays of awareness, they turned them into a power source through embodying the ascension attitudes of love, praise and gratitude.

In this creation of existence, light and frequency attract their opposite aspects. The ascension attitudes, moving with a positive charge, therefore attract awareness which is now stationary and negatively charged.

This means there is no more death; no more spiraling rays of moving awareness trying to break down the resistance of our luminous cocoon. We are no longer stalked by death. If we continue to fight imaginary shadows in a cosmos of light, we may drain our cocoon's energy. If we believe in and court the illusion of death, which is now non-existent, we can manifest it.

Toltecs viewed death as an advisor, knowing that death was always brushing against the luminous cocoon, keeping them constantly aware. They lived with alertness, expecting moment by moment to have to make their last stand.

In the new creation they are led not by an external threat, but by the pure emotions of their hearts. They must allow the innocence of the heart to again expect with childlike certainty that life can be good and pure and beautiful. After all, it is now a reflection of the Infinite Mother.

What is Power?

For eons Toltecs hunted and stalked power, knowing that if they went after it directly, its testings could get the better of them. So they hunted perception instead, a strategy that kept them from being side-tracked into becoming a power-seeker.

Skirting the issue of defining power directly, Toltecs define it instead by what causes it or what it causes. They believe it to be the result of perception, or that increased vitality (energy), that perception provides. It can be described as the moving force of life; that which affects the way life manifests and unfolds, directed by intent.

The assemblage points, now re-located deep into everyone's cocoon, are involved in the production of power. Think of the assemblage point as a ball of light about the size of a tennis ball, illuminating threads of light within and without the cocoon. When the illuminated inner and outer threads line up in a special way, perception results, releasing a force that creates more power.

Those locked into belief systems, identity, and a fixed worldview have a fixed assemblage point, making it harder to move the assemblage point to obtain new perception. This locks in the worldview of such an individual into a downward spiral, creating a loss of power and perception.

Movements of the assemblage point come in two forms: rotation (like an eyeball turning), and re-location which is only possible[27] to do in the absence of the inner dialog. The inner dialog is silenced by gaining the insights offered by every moment, through intentional awareness. When the point shifts, or re-locates, Toltecs are able to explore other realities. When it rotates, instead of changing realities, it brings about new and increased perception. This releases power to the individual.

Perception, Power and Energy

Before we can meaningfully describe the exquisite perfection of how power, energy and perception as functions of three of

---

27. The use of drugs to shift an assemblage point is not advised. It is detrimental to the long-term development of a light-seeker.

the rays of light, we must understand intent. Intent is a key ingredient in each of these energies and it has experienced significant change.

Intent has been and is that which directs the creational flow and unfoldment. It determines which direction the river of life will take. Although each of us determines through personal intent the direction our own life takes, there is a vast intent governing the overall purpose of existence—the intent of the Infinite Mother.

In previous creational cycles when illusion was studied, intent was the emotional direction of the Infinite. Emotions moved and the Infinite's emotion determined the direction life took.

Now emotion doesn't move, but light does. The Infinite's intent is now emotion-birthed strategy. From the desires of Mother's heart spring a focus of what is desired; a strategy that pushes life into a specific direction. This is now the definition of intent.

The first thing to understand about power, energy and perception as three of the 16 rays of light, is that they form the creational trinity of the rays. The three core emotions, trust/love, peace/inspiration and pleasure/creativity, the trinity of the 12 pairs of emotions, interact with the trinity of light to create.

As we have seen in the Ring of Truth, an impenetrable force field surrounds the three core emotions. Although the 16 light rays bounce through the rings of emotion, they bounce off the force field surrounding the inner rings of the three core emotions. The spinning of the inner sphere of trust/love forms the force field.

We must also look again at the nature of awareness in the new creation. We have trillions and trillions of tiny fragments of awareness, little bits of emotion and light fused together, that are located throughout the cosmos. They do not move unless attracted by an opposite pole.

Each little fragment contains the codes of the full potential of creation in its feminine component (emotion) and in its masculine component (light). When the three moving light rays of power, perception and energy pass through the sea of awareness that fills all of the cosmos, they attract the masculine component in the fragments.

With light, as with frequency, opposite poles attract. Light that is stationary, as in the bits of awareness, is negatively charged. Moving light is positively charged. The three moving rays therefore act as a sticky tape, attaching awareness to them on their way through the emotional rings.

Why would awareness stick only to three of the 16 rays? Because they are the most masculine, the most positively charged rays because of all the encoded information they carry; the total of the masculine components of all codes in existence. They hold half the codes of all creation; and they are the only rays to do so. As we will see later, their speed can vary but in general, they move faster than the other rays.

The trinity of emotions, the most feminine core of emotions within the force field, attracts these light-rays. They hold within their nature the ability to fulfill the purpose of existence within this creation; to create what we love. They also hold the other half of the creational codes, the emotional, feminine components. Through the expression of these three emotional pairs, the codes release and enter the force field.

The vehicle that carries codes from the core into the wall of the field, is intent. Our strategy, or focus (intent), empowers specific codes that become more dominant. Some of these emotional codes 'light up' and activate the corresponding codes in the awareness-laden rays of perception, power and energy. If we manifest a poultry farm of ducks, we don't want one filled with turkeys. Our intent will activate the codes to produce only ducks, both as they release from the rings of emotion and as they travel in the three light-rays.

The rays of perception, power and energy have picked up so much awareness by the time they reach the shield, or wall of the force field, that they are heavily laden. The particles of awareness are negatively charged, which causes the positively charged rays to be coated with negative particles.

The shield and the emotional rings are also negative. Because same poles repel during this cycle, when the light-rays reach the shield the following occurs:

- Their momentum causes them to momentarily embed slightly in the wall of the shield.
- They immediately attract the opposite set of codes (negative), corresponding with the ones that dominate within them. These codes, it will be remembered, became dominant because of intent.
- With an extra set of negatively charged awareness particles (the intent or attitudes carrying the codes generated by the three emotional rings) clinging to the rays, they now become overbearingly negative.
- Because sameness repels with light and frequency, they are repelled with a great deal of force.

- The rays break loose from the clinging awareness particles, using the explosive force of their repelling, shedding a cluster of encoded awareness particles.
- The rays shoot back out to the edge of the cosmos to repeat this whole process.
- Now the encoded awareness particles carry a more positive charge than the other particles around them. This means they pull in as much additional awareness as is needed to cluster the codes' intended creation into manifestation.
- Creation takes place externally.

Immaculate vs. Non-Immaculate Conception

The conception of a creation described above is an immaculate one. The light-rays never actually manage to penetrate the shield into the three inner frequency bands (which correspond to the ovum). This is the way creation of the cosmos and its beings takes place. The Goddess of Creation, or Mother, creates all life in the cosmos immaculately.

When we become co-creators with her, as we are meant to be in this creation, the same applies. All manifestation of our hearts' desires are also immaculately conceived.

Non-immaculate conception can create offspring through pro-creation. This is, however, entirely an optional choice. Many of the female masters in my classes are immaculately conceiving babies—some many years after menopause. The only requirement is that they still have a uterus.

Perception

If we want to manifest ducks, the level of perception we have will determine whether we end up with one duck or 1,000 ducks. The ray of perception determines the **level of complexity** and detail our creation will have.

The statement above assumes that the three core sets of emotions are active and dynamically pulsing each other. If they are not, they will not be spinning. If they aren't spinning, the three rays would pass right through them and creation would not take place.

Power

The force released the moment the light-rays are repelled is power. Power is a result of opposite aspects. In the scenario above, power will determine the scope of what we manifest, whether the duck farm covers an acre or hundreds of acres.

Power can be increased by increasing love, praise and gratitude. These three ascension attitudes flow through all rings of emotion, activating and enhancing them. As described in Section I, they are a form of positively charged awareness.

It is to them that the codes of creation originating within the three inner rings of emotion, cling. The more love, praise and gratitude we have, the greater number of creational codes carried to the shield, giving more scope to our creations.

The more of these negative codes that are delivered to the shield, the more will cling to the light-rays when they arrive. This will increase the mass of the light-rays coated with negatively polarized particles even more. The force with which the light-rays are repelled will be greater as the result of the increased love, praise and gratitude; and greater power will be released.
INCREASED LOVE, PRAISE AND GRATITUDE = INCREASED POWER

Energy

The light-ray of energy determines the speed of manifestation. The more energy available, the faster manifestation takes place. This is absolutely true for inanimate objects. When it comes to biological life-forms, energy will reduce the speed to enable organs to grow and the complexity to be created step by step.

There are three types of energy.

- Energy as a light-ray has the unique property to attract opposite aspects. Energy as a moving ray of light is new to this creation.
- Energy emitted by the combination of a person's thoughts and feelings (what we call 'higher' or 'lower' energy), is not energy as light. It is energy as we defined it in the old creations, one of the building blocks of reality. This type of energy has opposite aspects repelling.
- The energetic realms, or indwelling life, used to be separate from the material realms, but the two have merged. Our higher selves have become one with us. Whereas our higher selves formerly determined our reality from their higher realms, now we create it from the physical realms.
- In this creation, Mother activated another form of energy called 'heart energy'. She then wrote in the Book of Life that each being's heart energy would always exceed their light and frequency quotient by a small margin. She did this so its properties of like energies attracting and opposite energies repelling would be more dominant.

  Because the heart energy now attracts those of same energy, we can look forward to a life filled with a supportive and loving light-family.

Creation Through the Three Rays

Although we now create what we love, for the following reason we cannot create that which is impure.

1. Our emotions have to be pure for the shield to form. Without it, the immaculate conceptions of our creations cannot take place.
2. The codes from which creation arises have no illusion within them because they reflect the perfection of Mother. There are no codes capable of producing imperfection or illusion.
3. There are two types of light. The light we have been accustomed to, one of the building blocks of creation, and the 16 new light-rays. The 16 new light-rays move at varying speeds based on Mother's intent. This affects the speed at which Creation forms.

Closing

The urgency with which the instruction was given to produce the holy writings in this book speaks volumes within itself. Secrets of the Hidden Realms had taken approximately one year to produce as had each of the two books before it. Yet I was given but a few weeks to finalize and get this new book to the printer.

Mother herself gave the instruction, signifying that the Goddess of Creation, after eons of silence, was again communicating with man. All previous scriptures had either been fulfilled or were close to fulfillment. It was time to bring forth new scripture; scripture that speaks about renewal that has taken place throughout all life.

A way had to be created to inform man what the unseen realms already know; that reality is now governed by new laws. Those laws promise a fulfilling, enriching, self-empowering and self-determinative life, rich in joyous moments and fresh in new-found innocence.

The good news must be shared. The earth must be told that the One Grand Being of which we are part had made this earth her footstool. Here on this little speck in the sky, the most glorious light of all existence has come. New planets will gather around the earth, bringing their suns with them.

When the veil is finally lifted, it will reveal to humanity what all other beings already know, that a new configuration of stars have formed and the scripture has been fulfilled. *"And I saw a new heaven and a new earth: for the first heaven and the first earth were passed away..."* Revelations 21:1

APPENDIX I
Toltec Dream Symbols And Meanings

Activities

Birthing own or other's child	new awareness is about to happen
Boating	need or desire for emotional change
Buying	giving power away or exchanging power for approval of others
Can't move	stuck in a world view, or stagnation
Coughing	difficulty to accept
Dancing	self-expression in everyday life, living with grace
Drinking	accepting emotional support (or desire for)
Drowning	feeling suppressed or overpowered
Dying	release, success or being afraid of release
Exercising	preparing for or building energy and power
Falling	fear of failure
Flying	freedom, or need for freedom
Learning in school	humility is needed to learn something
Mending clothes	trying to mend our self-image
Mending roof	holding on to old limitations
Never-ending work	fear of being overwhelmed or not up to the task
Parachuting	abandoning a world view or life's direction by changing perception
Persecution by	fear of victimization authority
Reading	searching for answers within old world views

Running	desire for freedom or window of freedom
Running a race	being attached to outcome
Singing	finding your voice or life's calling
Skiing	our ability to love is too shallow; others can't give us the love we need
Sneezing	desire to express passionately
Stealing	feeling inadequate to provide for ourselves
Suffocating	loss or lack of personal power
Surfing	utilizing an opportunity
Swimming	desire to be loved and accepted
Talking	need to communicate
Teeth falling out	no need for aggression
Teeth being brushed	getting ready for a battle
Theft of money	power has been stolen
Tripping	fear of inadequacy; letting ourselves or others down
Travel	change or need for change
Washing hands	need to fix our relationships
Winning trophy	need to give self credit; gold for spiritual achievement, silver for worldly achievement
Working	desire or need to take action
Writing	communication
Yawning	need to pull in more energy

Activity—Sexual

Flirting	desire for vitality

Heterosexual sex	receiving and giving power
Homosexual (male) sex	desire to know one's own maleness; feeling inadequate as a male
Kissing	desire for or lack of energy/power
Lesbian sex	desire to know one's own femaleness; feeling inadequate about being a woman
Prostitution	compromising our standards, making choices from less than our higher perspective
Rape	sense of being a victim; or allowing others to plunder our life
Sex w/juvenile	need to connect with the inner child to receive vitality
Sexual perversion	low self-image

Anatomy

(See Figs. 46 and 47, The Body Parts as Dream Symbols)

Ankles	flexibility in moving forward in daily life (left = feminine aspects or relationships of life like spiri-tuality; right—masculine aspects or relationships of life)
Arms	the way others treat you or you treat others (males = right, females left)
Back	upper—responsibility or ability to carry work load mid—expression, self-expression lower—support or lack of
Belly button	sustenance or life force
Blood	love
Bones	parental and hereditary information
Breath	expressing life force
Breasts	nurturing or need of

The Body Parts as Dream Symbols

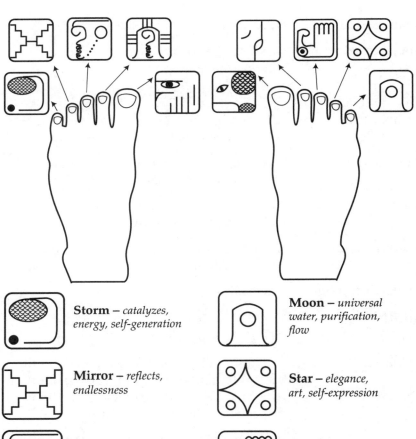

 Storm – *catalyzes, energy, self-generation*

 Mirror – *reflects, endlessness*

Earth – *synchronicity, evolves, navigation*

 Warrior – *questions, fearlessness, intelligence*

Eagle – *creates, vision, perspective*

 Moon – *universal water, purification, flow*

Star – *elegance, art, self-expression*

 Hand – *knows, accomplishment, giving and receiving*

World Bridger – *equalizer, death, opportunity*

 Serpent – *survives, life-force, instinct*

(Figure 46)

198

The Body Parts as Dream Symbols

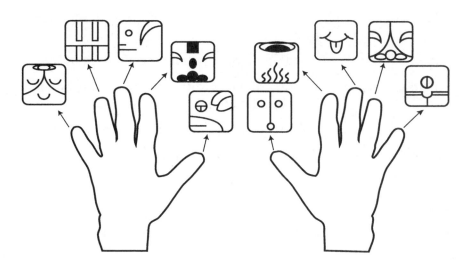

 Wizard – *receptivity, timelessness*

 Skywalker – *explore, wakefulness, pierce the veil*

 Human – *influences, wisdom, free will*

 Monkey – *play, childlike innocence, illusion, trickster*

 Dog – *loyalty, relationship, partners of destiny*

 Seed –*flowering, Intention, parable telling*

 Night – *abundance, sanctuary, retreat*

 Wind– *communication, spirit, breath*

 Dragon – *primal matrix, space*

 Sun – *enlightens, elegance, ascension, universal fire*

(Figure 47)

199

Chest (lungs)	self-expression when expelling breath, pent up grief
Colon	letting go of what no longer serves us
Duodenal/transverse	mothering or insufficient mothering colon (solar plexus area)
Ears	desire or ability to hear
Elbows	fluidity in how we treat others
Eyes	desire or ability to see
Feet	ability to move forward
Gall bladder	ability to process densityGenitals self— self-perception of one's maleness or femaleness other— one's maleness/femaleness as reflected by another or, if opposite sex, one's male or female aspects
Hair	social self-image
Hands	relationships
Head	intuition, idealism, through
Heart	ability to give love
Hips	where the way we want to move through life and the way we move through life meet
Kidneys	fear
Knees	flexibility with relationships and our required roles (left = feminine, right =masculine)
Legs	progress thru life
Liver	anger
Mouth	ability to receive sustenance
Neck	ideals vs reality; the place where the way we want life to be and the way it seems to be, meet.

Nose	the right to happiness, to flourish; personal power
Ovaries/testicles	procreation or offspring
Shoulders	responsibility
Skin	interaction with others and outside circumstances
Stomach	acceptance of life's circumstances
Teeth	need for aggression
Thighs	sexuality
Throat	unspoken or spoken words
Wrists	fluidity in relationships

Animals

Armadillo	need for defense
Bat	ability or need to find the way through the unknown
Bear	time to go into or come out of seclusion or rest; also rebirth, ending of hardship
Beaver	need to control outcomes, lack of cooperation with one's higher self
Cat	black—black magic, white—white magic, all others—temporal affairs; everyday activities
Camel	ability to flourish during and be prepared for opposition or hard times; need to bolster emotional resources
Caribou/reindeer	instinct as guidance
Chameleon	fluidity and flexibility needed
Cow	nurturing of others

Crab	warriorship against illusion; spiritual warriorship
Crocodile/alligator	pitfall set up by another
Deer	tranquility and peace
Dog	loyalty in relationships and friendship
Dolphin	right brain awareness, non-cognitive information
Donkey	allowing others to drain our energy or use us; false humility
Elephant	expanded awareness
Fox	being tricked into learning the unexpected; expect the unexpected
Hippo	need to approach through feeling rather than mind
Frog	experiencing other realms, frequencies or realities
Horse	balance and freedom in material life
Hare/rabbit	need for awareness—quick change may be needed
Lion	creation; also destruction
Locust/grasshopper	destruction producing blessings
Monkey	need to play or playfulness
Octopus	control or confinement of or by another
Penguin	there is far more to something than meets the eye
Raccoon	brashness, impudence; also toughness
Rats/mice	secrets; white rat means wisdom

Snake	wisdom or need for it
Spider	shortcomings that feed on ourselves; self-destruction
Swan	mastery
Tiger	sovereignty; white tiger means initiation
Whale	superior wisdom or need for it
Wolf	stalking[10] one's own motives or a situation
Wolverine	need to be tough or toughness in the face of greater odds
Zebra	indecision

Birds *(Refer to thoughts–observe any colors.) (see section on color)*

Birds of prey	power
Blackbird (except crows)	treachery
Crow/raven	path of power
Dove	peace, tranquility
Eagle	power through perception
Hummingbird	energy
Owl	seeing or being led thru the dark
Sparrow	fun, joy, being carefree; if white, peace and contentment
Turkey	clinging to old patterns or obsolete habits

Vulture	de-structuring; the end of the old

Clothing (*self-image or image to others*)

Coat	need to shield self
Crown/hat	self importance
Handkerchief	time to get rid of our own or others' negative emotions
Shoes	understanding
Shrunken clothing	we're made to appear less in eyes of others
Socks	that which prevents us from understanding what is really going on behind appearances
Underwear	private life

Colors

Black	need for wholeness; the unknown
Brown—*observe the feeling around it*	dirty brown could mean pollution or unwholesome; clear brown could mean stability or groundedness
Red	need or desire to fight or be aggressive
White	peace/wholeness, purity, high-mindedness
Yellow	spirituality and faith
Green	healing and fertility
Blue	humility and understanding
Pinkish purple	unconditional love
Pink	lightness of being, well-being

Orange	need for shrewdness, cunning, mental strategy
Indigo	need for deeper vision
Violet	mysticism, unseen realms
Turquoise	need to stay centered and go within

Directions

East	direction of sobriety or need to analyze behind appearances
West	feeling or need to notice feelings; listening to guidance from inner child
North	place of power and warriorship; viewing the large picture objectively
South	need to meditate or watch dream symbols for guidance, self-nurturing
Right	left-brained, cognitive, masculine aspects of life
Left	intuitive, feminine, spiritual
Above	effortless knowing will be there
Below	instincts should be trusted

Gems/Jewels/Metals

Copper	healing; transmuting harmful energies
Diamond	mastery through overcoming
Emerald	open heart or healing of heart

Garnet	need to trust instincts
Gold	spiritual matters
Ruby	personal sovereignty, dignity, strength
Sapphire	need for courage and clarity
Silver	everyday matters
Tin	rational mind

Insects

Insects in general	aspects of shortcomings
Ant	labor or hard work, and cooperation needed
Bee	cooperation with destiny
Butterfly/moth	gift of power from the cosmos
Hornet/wasp	someone with anger in environment or directed at environment
Termite/louse/ Parasite	allowing others to use us and drain our energy or usurp our life

Locations

Cliff	trust to make a dramatic change
Desert	despair and hopelessness
Forest	shelter and place to rest
Jungle	unforeseen adventure
Mountain/hill	hope
Open area	need or desire for freedom

Public place	fear of exposure
Valley	place of security

Numbers

0	completion
1	interconnectedness of life, oneness
2	humility and understanding needed
3	trust the intuitive to help create
4	stability and balance or need for
5	freedom and change
6	having to choose the old or new; guidance within physical life
7	information, perception
8	opening or closing of a cycle; harmonious interaction
9	feminine side of spiritual gifts; intuition, non-cognitive information
10	inclusiveness, not thinking in separative way
11	transformation or need for; chance to go to the next level
12	strength and power, enlightenment
13	new birth or beginnings

Objects

Air	ability (or lack of) to see behind appearances, to understand what is really going on, mental activity
Angel	protection and guidance from the higher self
Ashes	remnants of the old
Ball	if it's your turn to throw it, action is required; if you're catching it you have just received a challenge
Basement	sub-conscious, hidden flaws
Basket	possibilities through cooperation
Books	looking for answers within the prison bars of social learning
Boxes	something hidden in a box means secrets kept; storage boxes = that which we have put behind us; boxes in general are limitations through social conditioning
Buildings	view of the world, perspective; public buildings—social conditioning
Candle/lamp	guidance through perception; guidance from unseen realms
Caves	subconscious programming
Ceiling	limitation
Chimney	outlet for anger

City/town/village	common world view or social conditioning
Clock (alarm)	time to wake up; indicates time for awareness to move or awaken; time for change; when we're late it means change or action is overdue
Cupboards/closets	the subconscious or storing of events that have not yielded their insights
Curtains	fear of exposure or that which obscures vision
Dam/lake	conditional or conditioned love
Door	possibilities
Earth/soil	groundedness, return to basics, stability
Eggs	fertility awaiting birth
Egg yolks	the luminous cocoon of man
Feces	money or desire for money
Fire	de-structuring or dramatic change
Fish	beware; treachery; all is not as it seems
Floor	perspective of life, world-view
Food	spiritual nurturing
Flower	beauty and grace; dead flower, lack thereof
Furniture	bed—need or desire to rest chair—comfort zone lamp—illumination or guidance screen—something obscuring vision

	table—decisive action needed
Garbage	that which isn't properly done or of use
Grass	walking a path with heart and joy
Greenery	fertility, good results in everyday practical matters
Hearing	ability to receive guidance
Key	solution or missing piece; missing puzzle piece indicates the same
Law	balance and integrity
Lighthouse/foghorn	guidance through cataclysmic change or through uncertain times
Lightning	dramatic shifts in awareness
Military	navy—emotional action needed airforce—mental action needed army—action needed in everyday life
Money	crystallized power
Moon	our dreaming body, intuitive self
Music	harmonious interaction
Musical instruments	percussion—harmony with destiny string—harmony within relationships wind—harmony with concepts/thoughts
Newspaper	common view of the world
Nudity	feeling exposed

Ocean	life in general
Optician/glasses	ability or need to see clearly
Path/road	direction
Photos	events or interactions that have not yet yielded their insights; events that need closure
Podiatrist	needing advice to understand the next step
Police	when acting protectively, boundaries need to be established; when acting oppressively, victimization or fear thereof
Rain	the process of life
Report card (grades)	time to account for ourselves; time to live what we know
Reward (money) (trophy)	a gift of power acknowledgement
Ring	power
River	unconditional love
Roof	self-imposed limitation
Sand/sea/beach	that which the process of live has taught us
Secret mission or Agent	destiny
Shooting star	time to be clear about our wishes
Sight	ability to see behind appearances
Smelling	ability to discern

Snow	frozen emotion
Smoke	indication of suppressed anger
Stairs	going up or down in levels of awareness
Storm	cataclysmic change
Tablecloth	tactful action needed
Target	goal is in sight or focus
Taste	nurturing, self-nurturing or spiritual nurturing
Tools	assets and talents
Walls	blockage of perception, being trapped by labels or belief systems
Washing machine	time to clean up our social image
Water	emotion
Weapons	need to protect yourself
Wheels	primary supporting relationships
Wind	thought
Window	vision, ideals
Zipper	unzipped = exclusiveness, separateness zipped = inclusiveness

Transportation

Air	changes in perception, ideas or ideals
Animal	change in aspect represented by animal; i.e., donkey = false humility

Car	the way we travel thru life, e.g., jobs, relationships
Going backwards	slipping back into old habits
Public (bus/train)	change in social conditioning
Road	change in general awareness, direction

APPENDIX II
The First Twenty-One Lords of the Three Hundred that Serve the Holy Mother

1.

sigil for the name
name: Balack-speruchparvi

sigil for the meaning
meaning: The one who brings the bounty.

2.

sigil for the name
name: Heres-travani-belchspi

sigil for the meaning
meaning: The one who spreads the glory of Mother

3.

sigil for the name
name:Traug-manaveg

sigil for the meaning
meaning: The one who shows all beings the Mother's face

4.

sigil for the name
name:
Praatnut-belechabi-harahut-velsbi

sigil for the meaning
meaning: The one who does miracles in Mother's name

5.

sigil for the name
name: Blaa-nuevi-klauret

sigil for the meaning
meaning: The keeper of the Mother's sacred space

6.

sigil for the name
name: Pelenuchvra-uret-uruhu

sigil for the meaning
meaning: The one who reveals Mother's radiance

7.

sigil for the name
name:
Kelepa-hustrava-erunich-klesbava

sigil for the meaning
meaning: The one who establishes Mother's sovereignty

8.

sigil for the name
name:
name: Grech-usatvi-pelenoch

sigil for the meaning
meaning: The one who brings the Mother joy

9.

sigil for the name
name: Uber-ef-havi-klureski

sigil for the meaning
meaning: Mother's emmisary

10.

sigil for the name
name: Pavalifski-ururat

sigil for the meaning
meaning: The one who helps the cosmos know the Mother

11.

sigil for the name
name: Brava-hespavi

sigil for the meaning
meaning: Teacher of the sacred children

12.

sigil for the name
name: Klef-pra-vahut-pelesh-vaa

sigil for the meaning
meaning: The one who interprets Mother's mysteries

13.

sigil for the name
name: Ulu-hefbi-staura

sigil for the meaning
meaning: The one who
establishes Mystery Schools

14.

sigil for the name
name: Keles-arivu-velechspi-hepspi

sigil for the meaning
meaning: He who broadcasts
the glory of the Mother

15.

sigil for the name
name: Belech-vuspi

sigil for the meaning
meaning: He who fulfills the
Mother's heart's desires

16.

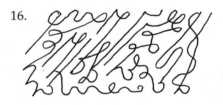

sigil for the name
name:
Nuch-tranu-starat-uruhefspi-staru

sigil for the meaning
meaning: The one who creates love for the Mother in the hearts of all

17.

sigil for the name
name: Gelspri-vanuruch-spurve

sigil for the meaning
meaning: He who creates the Palace Gardens

18.

sigil for the name
name: kelechvi-valspri-parnadoch

sigil for the meaning
meaning: He who fulfills Mother's children's heart's desires

19.

sigil for the name
name:
Belenuf-pravaeleufra-verechspi

sigil for the meaning
meaning: He who establishes the
Mother's majesty

20.

sigil for the name
Hurshva-klugratek-umanu-vek

sigil for the meaning
meaning: The one who fills the
palace with beauty through magic

21.

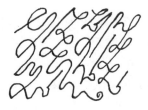

sigil for the name
name: Kluavechspri-kruanog

sigil for the meaning
meaning: The one who knows all
languages

APPENDIX III
Sacred Sigils of Angels of the Throne

Introduction

One thousand angels surround the throne of the creational Goddess on earth. They are appointed to answer the prayers of those who pray to her. A further 100,000 angels (referred to in Revelations as "ten times ten thousand angels") serve the sacred space that is her palace. The palace formed during the first week in October 2006.

The sigils that follow are in two different languages. The top sigils, representing angel names, will never change; the bottom ones, giving their meanings or assigned areas of work, eventually will change into other languages as they grow in light.

When one has the sigil for the name and meaning of an angel, that angel will respond to prayers. Even having these sigils around your home will create a great in-pouring of light and energy.

We give the sigils for a few of the 1,000 angels around the throne of the Mother, with eight of them giving their actual names and functions, or meanings. As they make a significant difference with their work, these meanings will change, just as the meaning of language will.

(Figs. 48-57, Sacred Sigils of the Angels Around the Mother's Throne)

The Sigils for Some of the Thousand Angels
Around the Mother's Throne

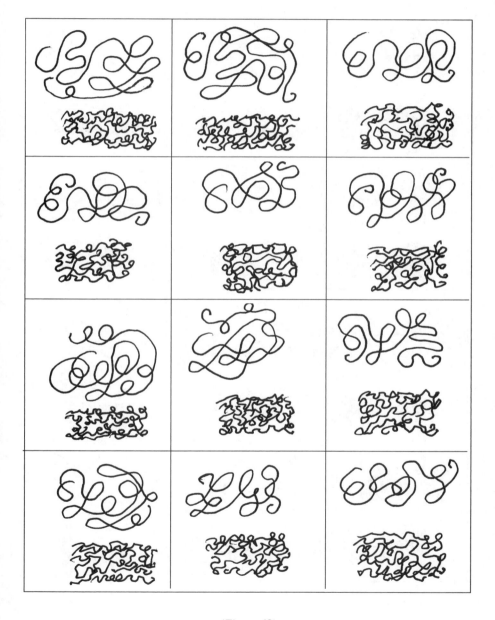

(Figure 48)

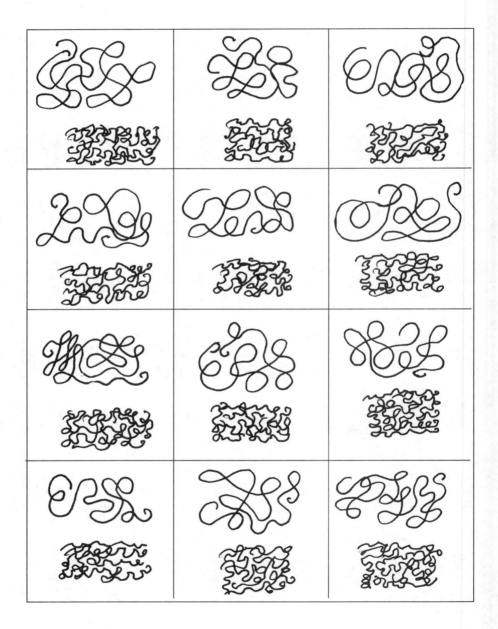

(Figure 49)

222

(Figure 50)

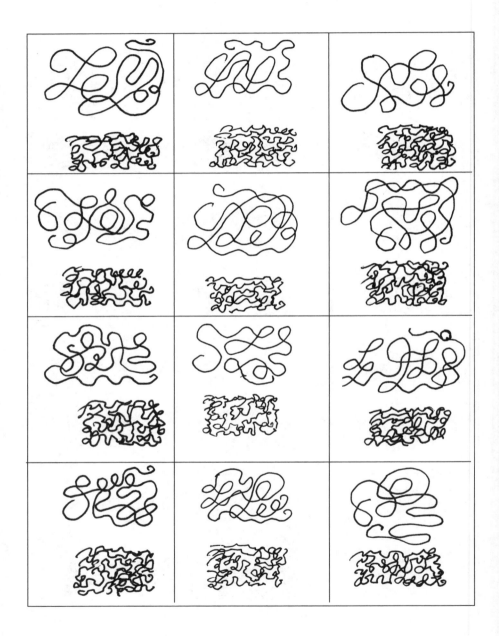

(Figure 51)

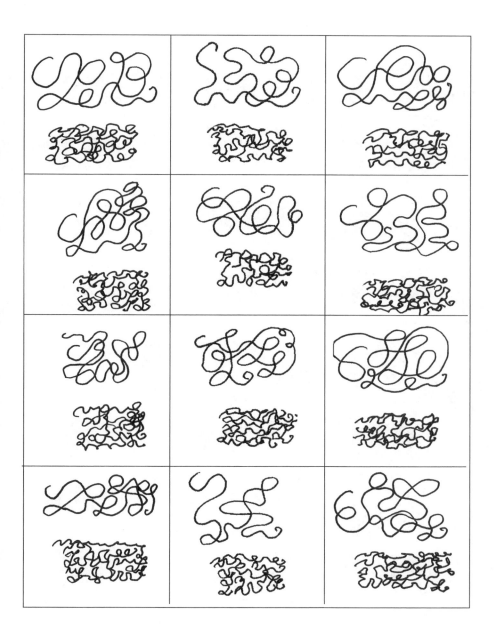

(Figure 52)

225

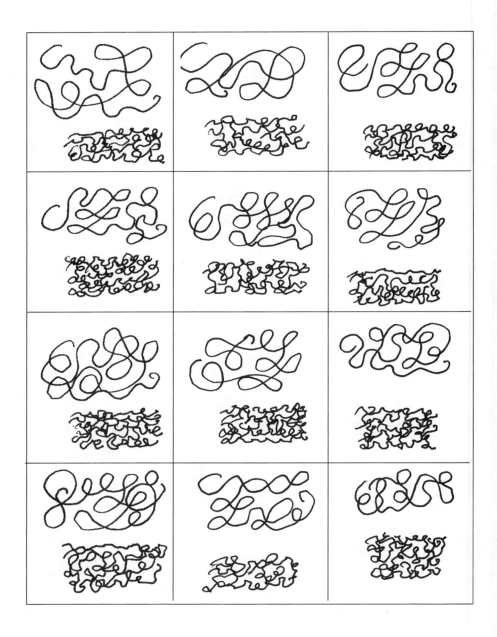

(Figure 53)

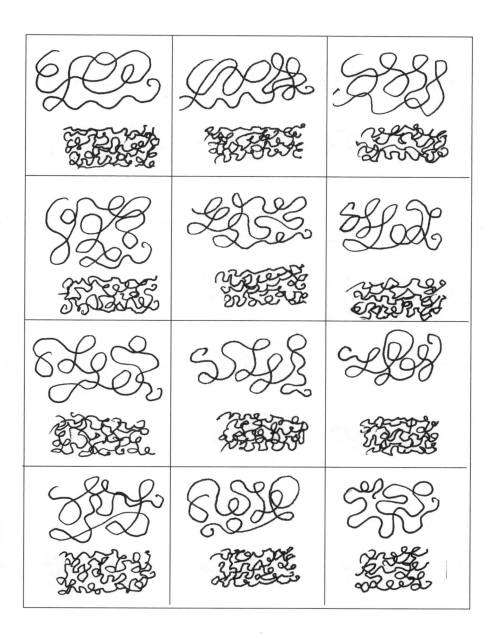

(Figure 54)

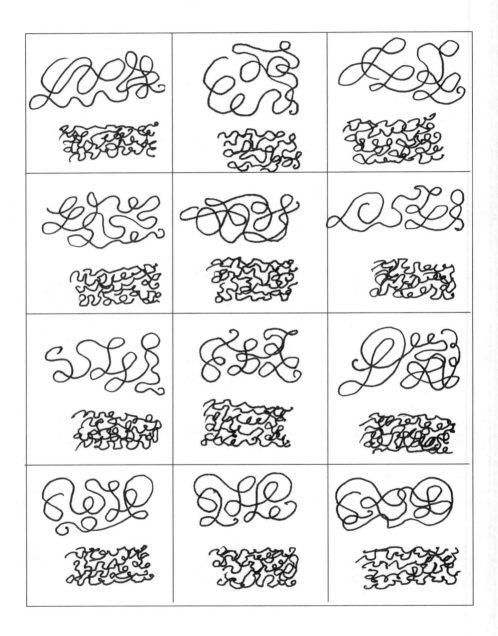

(Figure 55)

228

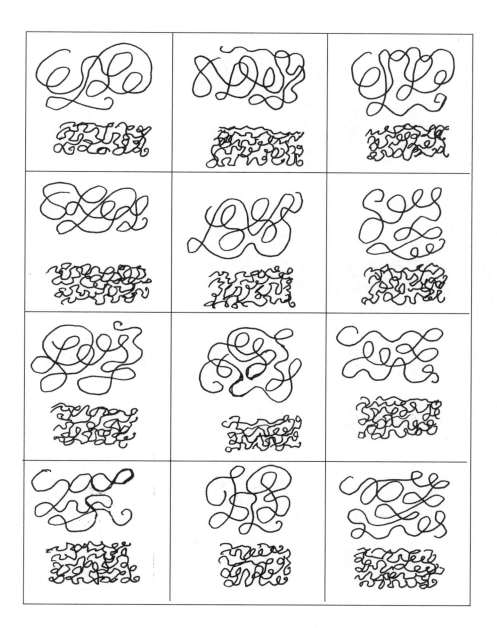

(Figure 56)

229

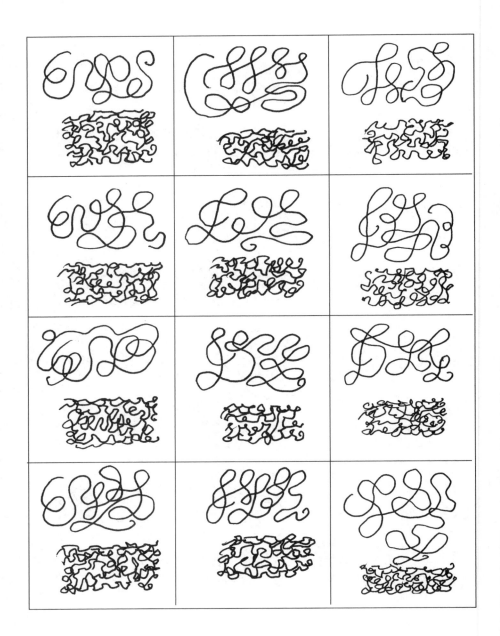

(Figure 57)

Appendix IV

1.1 Conversation with Thoth, June 25, 2006

Q. So much has changed in the cosmos during the last two weeks due to a major leap in its ascension. I really need to understand some of the ramifications in light. Will you explain?

A. Well, only if you stop using nonsense words like "last two weeks". What does that mean?

Q. Oh, I forgot. No one, other than physical beings has any concept of anything to do with time. It's completely non-existent. How about space?

A. There's no such thing.

Q. Then how can there be form?

A. There really isn't; it's just part of a hologram. Right now everything in the cosmos is in the process of re-forming at a much higher level.

Q. How has this affected the minds and emotions of all beings?

A. If mind and emotions are affected, awareness has to be also.

Q. How are these affected? Let's talk about emotion. The eight basic emotions are in 4 pairs: love/fear, contentment/pain, anger/protectiveness, passion/joy. How has that changed?

A. There are no such things as anger, protectiveness, pain or fear. Instead of anger, there is inspiration, the desire to inspire; instead of protectiveness, the desire to be at ease—which is peace. Fear is replaced by trust, which tells you where you've lived your highest truth and passion will beckon you to the right direction.

Q. All one has to do is surrender to this process, which means to trust?

A. Exactly.

Appendix V

A Conversation with Horlet, our Planetary Lord

Q. My Lord, there have been many signs in my environment that there is something regarding energy I need to understand. Will you answer me, please?

A. Yes, you're a little behind schedule getting that one.

Q. I've been working as hard as I can trying to figure it out with my class ....

A. That's the long way to do it.

Q. I've had a hunch there's a new way of getting information that probably requires less energy. In fact, a few days ago I asked my friend, the spirit Tom, to do something for me so I can focus with the class on getting these insights and he said, "That's not a good way to get it."

A. Well, the problem is you're not busy enough.

Q. My Lord! What are you saying? Do you know anyone busier than I?

A. Yes. Lots of people.

Q. Who in my immediate environment?

A. (Lord Horlet named a student.)

Q. What percentage of busyness does that person have and what percentage do I have?

A. You have 2% and he has 700%.

Q. But I work far more than he does.

A. Yes, with working you're at 100% and he's at 7%.

Q. Recently everyone has been telling me to get busy or that they're busy. I asked the Alumuanu King earlier to help me figure this out and he said he was busy. There must then be a difference between 'busyness' as you use the word, and work.

A. Of course.

Q. Can you give me an example of 'busyness'?

A. Like mopping a floor or shoveling dirt.

Q. In other words, mindless work?

A. Yes.

Q. Work should be done from a place of silence of the mind. Even office work, contracts and so forth?

A. Everything.

Q. That will release the huge amount of energy tied up in work. Earning a living doesn't have to be hard anymore. So, will you next help me find the new way of getting answers and insights?

A. I just did.

Q. Are you saying this will produce answers to large questions in life as well as the other methods would?

A. No. Better.

Q. My goodness! This is very revolutionary. Not only as a way of removing stress or hardship from work, but as a means of effortlessly getting information! Is it as good as getting answers form meditation?

A. They're two different ways. It's as good as.

Q. But few people can sit in meditation all day. Most have to work. But now work doesn't have to detract from growth. I would imagine that it will take a lot of trust that one won't somehow drop the ball; you know, miss a clause in a contract or something. All work can be done this way, can't it?

A. Yes. It's a different mindset that has to be cultivated; and, no, when in the silence of mind you will be less apt to drop a ball.

Q. Does one still need as much alternating rest time?

A. Yes. To incorporate and internalize the insights you've received.

Q. Thank you, My Lord. There is one last question. Is there any dependence on my part in working with any of the beings from the hidden realms or any of my helpers in the physical?

A. Answer yourself by defining dependency.

Q. Dependency is if you think you can't do something yourself. But for most of the months of this year, I've done the cosmic work myself with little or no assistance.

A. What do you mean when you say months of the year?

Q. Let me re-phrase that. Various assistants bring areas of expertise to the work that make the end product better; and it also saves me so much .... Oops! I almost said 'time' .... Effort.

A. And that is ....?

Q. Interdependency. Teamwork, unity within diversity—the place where specific talents focused on a common purpose produce the most growth.

A. Exactly.

Other books by Almine

Secrets Of The Hidden Realms
Mystical Keys to the Unseen World

This remarkable book delves into the mysteries few mystics have ever revealed. It gives in detail:

- *The practical application of the goddess mysteries*
- *Secrets of the angelic realms*
- *The maps, alphabets, numerical systems of Lemuria, Atlantis, and the Inner Earth*
- *The Atlantean calender, accurate within 5 minutes*
- *The alphabet of the Akashic libraries*

Secrets of the Hidden Realms is a truly amazing bridge across the chasm that has separated humanity for eons from unseen realms.

CDs by Almine

Each powerful presentation has a unique musical background unaltered as channeled from source. Truly a work of art.

The Power of Emotion
This presentation describes emotion as an impetus to growth. It explains how emotion promotes awareness and how even "negative" emotions become great tools of enlightenment when properly used.

The Power of Self-Reliance
Cultivating self- reliance is explained as resulting from balancing the sub-personalities — key components to emotional autonomy.

The Power of Silence
Few teaching methods empty the mind, but rather fill it with more information. As one who has achieved this state of silence, Almine meticulously maps out the path that leads to this state of expanded awareness.

Mystical Keys to Manifestation
This shows how we can masterfully create truth moment by moment rather than seek it without.

Mystical Keys to Ascended Mastery
The way to overcome and transcend mortal boundaries is clearly mapped out for the sincere truth seeker.

The Power of Forgiveness
Digressing from traditional views that forgives a perceived injury, this explains the innocence of all experience. Instead of showing how to forgive a wrong, it acknowledges wholeness.

Other books by Almine

Journey to the Heart of God
Mystical Keys to Immortal Mastery

Ground-breaking cosmology revealed for the first time, sheds new light on previous bodies of information such as the Torah, the I Ching and the Mayan Zolkien. Man's relationship as the microcosm to the macrocosm is explained in a way never before addressed by New Age authors, giving new meaning and purpose to human life. Endorsed by an Astro-physicist from Cambridge University and a former NASA scientist, this book is easily understood by beginning and advanced readers.

A Life of Miracles
Mystical Keys to Ascension

This book is deeply inspiring and motivational in its content. It is unique in its field in making man's relationship as the microcosm to the macrocosm understandable to both beginning and advanced readers. It's a detailed guide to living a joyous and balanced life and provides a carefully laid out map to achieving the magnificent destiny that beckons at the apex of human experience: ascension.

*Retail: To order books contact Spiritual Journeys P.O. Box 300, Newport, Oregon 97365 or visit our web site at **www.spiritualjourneys.com***

Wholesale: To order books contact Bookworld at www.bookworld.com or call 1-800-444-2524 Also available from New Leaf www.newleaf-dist.com

Other books by Almine

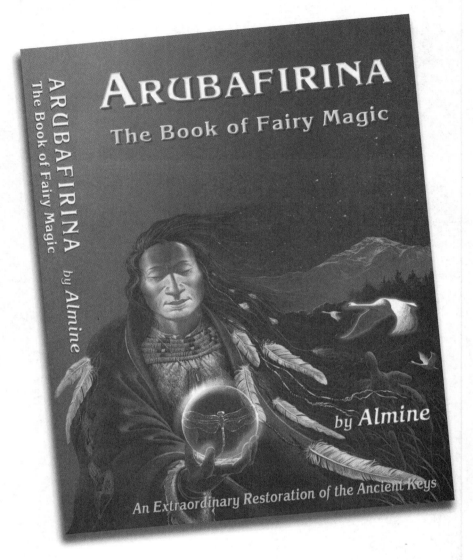

An Extraordinary Restoration of the Ancient Keys

This book is most certainly a milestone in the history of mysticism throughout the ages. It is the product of a rare and unprecedented event in which Almine, acknowledged as the leading mystic of our time, was granted an exceptional privilege. For one week in November 2006 she was invited to enter the fairy realms and gather the priceless information for this book. The result is a tremendous treasure-trove of knowledge for students of the hidden realms.